THE WRITER'S MENTOR

THE WRITER'S MENTOR

Secrets of Success from the World's Great Writers

Ian Jackman

editor

RANDOM HOUSE
REFERENCE

New York

The Writer's Mentor

This book is available for special discounts for bulk purchases for sales promotions or premiums. Special editions, including personalized covers, excerpts of existing books, and corporate imprints, can be created in large quantities for special needs. For more information, write to Special Markets/Premium Sales, 1745 Broadway, MD 6-2, New York, NY, 10019 or e-mail *specialmarkets@randomhouse.com*.

Please address inquiries about electronic licensing of reference products, for use on a network or in software or on CD-ROM, to the Subsidiary Rights Department, Random House Reference, fax 212-572-6003.

Visit the Random House Reference Web site: www.randomwords.com

Cover design by Nora Rosansky
Interior design by Tina Malaney

Typeset by North Market Street Graphics
Typeset and printed in the United States of America.

Library of Congress Cataloging-in-Publication Data

The writer's mentor : secrets of success from the world's great writers /Ian Jackman, editor.—1st ed.
     p. cm.
  ISBN 0-375-72061-8 (alk. paper)
    1. Authorship. I. Jackman, Ian.

PN147.W689 2004
808'.02—dc22

1st Edition

0 9 8 7 6 5 4 3 2 1

2004

0-375-72061-8

Contents

INTRODUCTION

New York City, Tuesday, September 2, 6:11 P.M. The Writer's Mentor *is falling into place, I think. It had better be, because today, for the second time, I e-mailed my editor to say that I wasn't quite finished, not just yet. Sorry. But another few days would do it, for sure. How about Friday? And I do mean it, but I haven't even started the introduction and this is the hardest part of the book because it is actual* writing. *The rest of the book has organized itself, by and large, but this is different. It's a blank page and nobody can help.*

A couple of times, when out on a run, I've had an idea of how to start. The first time, I'd run out of gas and was walking along under a hot sun. I'd overambitiously told my family I'd meet them at the beach, I had three miles to go and no company but my thoughts. What about that introduction?

With a minuscule leap of imagination, I thought, well, "Writing is like running." How about that? Each activity can appear easy, even effortless, yet neither is either of these things. Both require training, or practice at least. But the simile, like the runner, lacked legs. Sprints and marathons aren't analogous to poems and novels. Fitness, age, and physical ability don't fit well with the writing metaphor. It was a bad idea, but at least it was an idea.

And today, another run and another idea: "Writing is like juggling." I was thinking about Stephen King writing On Writing. *What can the man who can juggle eight balls teach someone unable to cope with three? An individual with such prodigious talents is wasting his time on journeymen like us, the thought went. His book would be an act of cruelty, like that of Ted Williams when he wrote* The Science of Hitting, *contending he could help you hit a baseball, if the advice in it weren't so down-to-earth and practical.*

The juggling analogy is more promising than the running one, but I don't want to go in that direction anymore. Instead, I want to write an introduction about the process of writing. By the time I near home at the end of my run, my mind is popping with this thought. I want to look at my notes and sit down and write them up. These ideas had been percolating, I realize, and I have to sit down, play with them, and see if there is anything there.

And now it is 6:54. The blip of opportunity is past because dinner is ready. There'll be rewriting, of course, and the aforementioned editor may throw out this conceit. I've been up from my chair at least eight times in forty-three minutes— fetching drinks of water, bathroom breaks, intercessions between the children, two trips to the same bag to fetch books I didn't need and one visit, unaccountably, to look in the mirror to make sure my eyebrows weren't out of whack. But this has been a start, right? So I go and open the notebook. I haven't looked at it for a while. I read "August 27; 3:42 P.M. Nicholson Baker's U and I is a book I like a lot."

I remember enjoying Nicholson Baker's *U and I*, his book about himself and John Updike. Once I've finished a book, my memory of it can be vague immediately, as if I hadn't being paying adequate attention while I was reading. It might be ten years since I read *U and I*, so before I've had a chance to find my copy of the book, what I think I recall is that Baker begins by setting out exactly how much of each of Updike's books he's actually read. Some he's finished; others he's read nothing of whatsoever. That's what I remember, but I can't be certain.

I thought of *U and I* because Baker's humility, or mock humility, was a potential model for this prefatory piece to *The Writer's Mentor*. I felt it would be better to talk about my writing experience in the same way that Baker had fessed up to the gaps in his reading of his subject's books. It seemed appropriate, somehow, like asking for credit for showing the working of a math puzzle when I couldn't quite come up with the answer.

Not that I don't have any experience. Rather, up to now, it's been concentrated in specialized areas of the publishing business. I've written part or all of a number of books of my own and other people's that total a little less than ten. In eight years and four months at Random House, I edited a larger number of books and watched many others being published, some of which were sent on their way with some form of blurb, cover copy, or other sales material penned by me. Amid this writing and ghostwriting, copywriting and editing, slush-pile reading and proposal formation, I can spot when a writer knows what she's talking about when she talks about writing—which is what, as editor of this volume, I hope I have achieved.

I first thought about roping in *U and I* on a New York City subway train, a Bronx-bound Number 9 train, to be precise. Why Nicholson Baker and *U and I* came into my head, I can't say, but they did, between 86th Street and 96th Street. It was before the rush hour and I had a seat. I'd been working, so I had my notebook and pen with me. I took the opportunity to write what was coming into my head. I started scrawling in my notebook. "Nicholson Baker's *U and I* is a book I like a lot." And I noted the day and time for good measure: 3:42 P.M.; August 27.

I wrote other notes as well. They were telling me that I could write the introduction and intercede with italicized comments, like thought balloons in a cartoon. "*Note to Ed.—is this okay?*" *I thought it might be necessary to have and reject a number of ideas (six ideas? ten?) before I had one that stuck.* "Ideas are a dime a dozen," I read that day. "It's part of the process," I wrote, meaning the having of the idea. "What got me to this."

Good stuff or bad, I was writing quickly. So much was I concentrating on the task that I missed my stop. Because there was construction on the line and some stations were being skipped, I looked up and I'd overshot my intended destination by three stations. I got out at 137th Street, took a free transfer and walked across Broadway for the trip back downtown. When I got on the next train I wrote, "*The run, the percolate,* [sic] *the procrastinate* [sic]. *The Time* [triple underscore] *finding the time.*"

I remembered reading what someone had written about ideas brewing, although I didn't think enough of it to make a note of the reference. It seemed to me that perhaps my first idea had been agitating and suddenly begotten a slew of other ideas. Also, I was now concentrating on the concept of having the time to write. You have to be receptive to ideas coming to you but it is essential to create the time to articulate the idea, write it down, and expand upon it. Otherwise it will be gone like the dream you half-remember on waking and lose in a careless instant. This might be the best advice I can offer: *Always carry a notebook and something to write with.* Without my notebook, I never would have tried to hold the thought.

Before I got to 116th Street, I wrote three words in a stack: "*Talent*"; "*Time*"; and "*Inclination.*" Okay, I agree that the writer needs these, but the order in which they appear should be reversed. If you have an inclination to write, you have to find the time to exercise it and then you'll find out if you have a talent for it. "*You'll never know if you don't try.*" But again, I was more struck by the presence of the idea than by any veracity it might or might not have. I was thinking about writing, and about writing a quite specific piece.

I had known for months that I would be writing something on these pages but had only focused on it recently. Then, in twenty minutes, an outline had presented itself. Of course, the writing and rewriting of it would take considerably longer.

Another scribble was about the necessity of reading. If I had never read *U and I*, it would never have occurred to me that the book might offer a solution to my problem writing this introduction. Or at least an idea as to where I might start to seek a solution. When writers write about writing, they are sure to discuss their reading. ("My friends turned me on to Kierkegaard, Beckett, Doris Lessing," writes Anne Lamott.) Of course, when I remembered *U and I*, I was a little sketchy about the details.

I found my copy of Baker's book where I thought it might be, at the back of a particular triple-stacked shelf. A 1991 Random House hardcover, and a first edition, I was pleased to see, no doubt purloined soon after I went to work at Random House in 1992.

I opened the book and soon found Baker's list of Updike's books. It wasn't at the start of the book though, but on pages 30–31. It begins,

"And yet, shockingly, I've read fewer than five pages of:

Rabbit Is Rich
Buchanan Dying
S.

Tossing and Turning
Telephone Poles"

And concludes,
"And I've read most or all of:

Pigeon Feathers
Of the Farm
The Poorhouse Fair
Rabbit, Run
Rabbit Redux
The Music School
Museums and Women
The Same Door"

For what it is worth, and it is nothing, it turns out that I have done about as well, or poorly, as Mr. Baker, as far as reading John Updike is concerned. But I soon realized, skimming through the book, that I was missing the point, or misre-membering it. Baker's homage is what the book jacket calls a *tour de force*. Baker's own brilliance can't be thrown entirely into the shadows by Updike's. The amount of his reading doesn't matter; it's a red herring.

I can say that I've looked at parts of a lot of books for *The Writer's Mentor*. While Nicolson Baker was reading novels, for the most part, many of the (nonfiction) books I used had indexes, I'm glad to say. If not, they at least were divided into parts, which allowed me to focus my reading.

I'll admit I was surprised at the tonnage of books about writing. Many are level-headed and offer sensible, practical advice. If a writer pens a memoir, she'll discuss her process. It is always fun to read about the often ritualized behavior of working writers. There is clearly no one right way to go about this.

Online, there is separate, and huge, cache of information that might look like another bounty. As with much on the Web, however, much of what is there is in the form of the vanity project. What seems to be so much is too much—the deficit by surfeit. The excellent *Writer's Digest* site is an exception. In the main, I used the Internet for writer's interviews; books for the rest.

The intention of this book is to show how other writers, including writers who have written about writing, have found success. These quotations are intended to suggest avenues you might want to explore further. If you like something someone says, check out the rest of his or her book. Bibliographical information is supplied at the end of this book.

I have quoted more of the books I liked better. Betsy Lerner's *The Forest for the Trees* gave the advice that made the most sense; Wallace Stevens's *Letters* was the most pleasurable book to read. I also liked Joyce Carol Oates's *The Faith of a Writer*, especially the sections on inspiration and failure. I don't hold with 100 percent of the advice quoted, but writing is such a difficult and slippery task that anything that worked for any of us bears consideration by all of us. This reader doesn't find most strict, directional advice about writing to be particularly useful. Likewise anything too "inspirational." You may feel differently.

Writing for children is beyond our ken. So is humor writing. Writers are either funny or they aren't, intentionally or otherwise. I'd just say I enjoyed *Me Talk Pretty One Day* by David Sedaris or *Oh, the Things I Know* by Al Franken and leave it at that.

The online world is little covered. Book publishers have long known that the Internet will transform their business, but with many misadventures in electronic publishing behind them, they appear no closer to figuring out how to be in the vanguard of that movement. Writers can now disseminate their work easily online, but publication in the more traditional sense of the word (that is, on paper) remains the goal of most writers, even if this is the last generation for whom that might be the case.

So *The Writer's Mentor* is a starting point in your investigation of the world of writing. Mentors don't prescribe. They don't have all the answers, but they know the right questions to ask. They nudge and suggest, pointing this way and that, all the while offering a kindly word in your ear.

◎ ◎ ◎

Wednesday, September 3, 12:56 A.M. The first draft is done, almost, and the time I am spending on it is bringing less and less reward the deeper into the rainy night I keep working. I hadn't remembered correctly how Nicholson Baker started U and I. *It was not, as I've mentioned, the list of Updike books he had and hadn't read. Happily for my purposes, it was more prosaic, and it was about process and writing about writing. Which was where we came in.*

On August 6, 1989, a Sunday, I lay back as usual with my feet up in a reclining aluminum deck chair padded with blood-

dotted pillows in my father's study in Berkeley (we were house-sitting) and arranged my keyboard, resting on an abridged dictionary, on my lap. I began to type the date and time, 9:46 A.M. I had no idea what subject I was going to cover that morning.

Am I wrong in thinking this comes from a similar constellation of ideas as my idea, if presented with an altogether brighter luminescence? After all, the next sentence mentions Baker having just sent off his second novel, Room Temperature, *but still, I'm allowing myself to be pleased. Fourteen years, twenty-one days, and six or so hours after Nicholson Baker, I'd written down a date and time and started my piece of prose. If that was good enough for the author of* U and I, *this is good enough for me.*

New York City
September 5, 2003

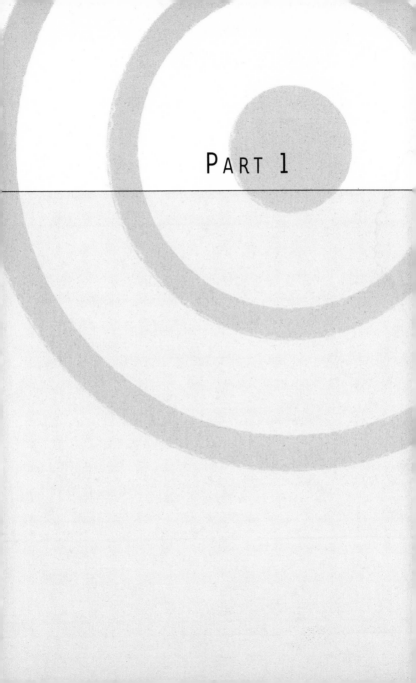

PART 1

INSPIRATION

"I once scribbled 'hobbit' on a blank page of some boring school exam paper in the early 1930s. It was some time before I discovered what it referred to!"
—J. R. R. Tolkien

"Writing is finally a series of permissions you give yourself to be expressive in certain ways. To invent. To leap. To fly. To fall."
—Susan Sontag

You want to write and you've found the time. Now you're staring at the blank page. It is unforgiving. You need *inspiration*.

At the age of eight, Ernest Gaines picked cotton and potatoes in the fields of Louisiana. As a teenager he moved to California, found a library, and read. He read books about what he called "peasant life": John Steinbeck on Mexicans in the Salinas Valley; Willa Cather on the Nebraska pioneers; Chekhov on Russian farm laborers; De Maupassant on French rural life. Reading these books made Gaines want to write, but he was inspired by what he *wasn't* reading. "I wanted to see something about my own people and there were no such books in that library." He wrote to put "the book there that was not there." Gaines has since written at least ten novels, many of which are set in America's south.

The yearning to be represented has inspired countless writers, whether they find their outlet in fiction or a memoir. The late novelist Carol Shields sought women she could recognize in the books she read, but found none. She set about creating her own characters because "Women in fiction were either bimbos or bitches."

Chinua Achebe grew up in Nigeria. His writing has been informed by what he sees as misrepresentations of the Africa he knew. Speaking at his induction to the American Academy of Arts and Sciences in 2002, Achebe described how non-Africans like Hemingway could write stories in which Africans would be little more than bystanders. "What African writers do," he said, "is take stories of Africa written by Westerners and stand them on their head." He continued:

> "If you read the kinds of books I read growing up, in which savages, African savages, are presented, you will remember that they have no speech. They howl or they screech. Make all kinds of other noises. What I heard growing up in my village was different. And that's what I write about."

Achebe has also spoken about the book that was his one of his inspirations, Joyce Cary's *Mister Johnson* (1939) based on the Anglo-Irish writer's experiences in Nigeria:

> "What *Mister Johnson* did do for me was not to change my course in life and turn me from something else into a writer;

I was born that way. But it did open my eyes to the fact that my home was under attack and that my home was not merely a house or a town but, more importantly, an awakening story in whose ambience my own existence had first begun to assemble its fragments into a coherence and meaning; the story I had begun to learn consciously the moment I descended from the lorry that brought me to me father's house in Ogidi; the story that, seventeen years later at the university, I still had only a sketchy, tantalizing knowledge of, and over which even today, decades later, I still do not have sufficient mastery, but about which I can say one thing: that is not the same story Joyce Cary intended me to have.

For me there are three reasons for becoming a writer. The first is that you have an overwhelming urge to tell a story. The second, that you have intimations of a unique story waiting to come out. And the third, which you learn in the process of becoming, is that you consider the whole project worth the considerable trouble—I have sometimes called it terms of imprisonment—you will have to endure to bring it to fruition. For me, those three factors were present, and would have been present had Joyce Cary never been born, or set foot in Nigeria. History, however, had contrived a crossing of our path, and such crossings may sometimes leave their footmarks, faint or loud, on memory. And if they do, they should be acknowledged."

The inspiration is the writer's sense of self—it comes *from* him or her, or it is *of* him or her. It is axiomatic that first novels often are autobiographical. Even the most fantastic created realms are conceived in the here-and-now.

Writers look for their own reality, however unusual or

deranged it may be. At some point, they begin to assess and elaborate upon their experiences not simply as an observer or a participant but as a *writer*.

The poet William Stafford has described the process of waiting for the idea to present itself.

> "Last night, sleeping on the floor of the Episcopal Church at Valdez, I dreamed that some old, exposed roll of film had turned up. I held it, ready to develop it, and thought of the scenes, the people, ready there to be mine again, from the vivid, precious past. Without knowing just what they would be I yet hungered for them all.
>
> "Writing is like that, I realize: to hold the pen and wait, then start, is like holding that roll of film. Something will come; it will bring from the past. I wait deliciously. And the thing that occurs depends partly on how much I hunger."

You start to be receptive to the idea of your own experience as a source.

> "I'm a journalist. I've always been a journalist. My books couldn't have been written if I weren't a journalist because all the material was taken from reality." —Gabriel García Márquez

> "My writing forces me to remember, because that is the source of my stories. If only I could create fiction out of the present, but the present is sacred to me, to be lived, to be passionately absorbed but not transfigured into fiction, to be preserved faithfully in the diary. The alchemy of fiction is, for me, an act of embalming." —Anaïs Nin

"One needs inspiration to write when one is twenty. At the age of sixty, there's the mess of one's entire life and little time remaining to worry about." —Charles Simic

"I wrote in-house brochures for Nabisco. It contributed to my poetry and life by instructing me exactly what I didn't want and couldn't bear." —Stephen Dunn

Joyce Carol Oates told the *New York Times*,

"The serious writer, after all, bears witness. The serious writer restructures 'reality' in the service of his or her art, and surely hopes for a unique esthetic vision and some felicity of language; but reality is always the foundation, just as the alphabet, in whatever motley splendor, is the foundation of *Finnegans Wake*."

When a writer is looking for something to write about, he or she often alights on that which is nearest to hand, namely the self. It's natural and obvious—we know ourselves, or we suppose we do, and our memories are a ready pool of images and sensations and stories. A writer might be prompted by a hope of redeeming some part of him- or herself.

"Writing is a second chance at life. Although we can never go back in time to change the past, we can re-experience, interpret, and make peace with our past lives." —Jane Taylor McDonnell, *Living to Tell the Tale*

"The memoirist takes a slice of life, a remembered image, and chews on it, munching slowly, if not perhaps deliberately,

There might well be some painful event or relationship you want to confront on paper. But think—if publication is your ultimate goal, do you really want anyone else reading what you intend to write? And if you don't mind, what makes your story different? What sets it apart from any other? At this juncture in the twenty-first century, we are jaded. We've read it all before. It puts a lot of pressure on the quality of your writing if you choose to write about yourself.

> **"If you write about your father hitting you on the head, you're up against a lot of competition with people who are writing about exactly the same experience. I used to tell students not to use certain subjects they seemed to gravitate to almost automatically at their age, such as the death of their grandparents—grandparents tend to die when you're in high-school or college. I at least want to read about something I don't already know about."** — John Ashbery

> **"When Muhammad Ali said, 'I am the Greatest,' he got away with it because he said it with a twinkle in his eye. Learning to write about yourself and your life so the twinkle in your eye shows is our mission."** —Lou Willett Stanek

to extract as much nutrition—as much meaning—from it as possible." —Maureen Murdock, *On Memoir and Memory*

Of course, you're in charge and you're making up the rules so you can set the out-of-bounds markers where you will:

"When I'm writing about myself I think about myself as a character. There is a ton of stuff going on in my life that I don't write about. If I need to write that stuff down, I write about myself in my diary." —David Sedaris

If you are writing for yourself or for your family, you won't be burdened by the problem of finding an audience for your work.

As for *where* to look,

"Writers almost always write best what they know, and sometimes they do it by staying where they know it. But not for safety's sake." —Eudora Welty

Inspiration is an abstract notion. At some point, a concrete idea must arise and take form, even if it comes during the writing. There will be a premise for the book or the story or the poem. Plot-driven novelists like thriller or mystery writers need an abundance of stories. They might take their professional experiences and decide to pour them into fiction; among these are writers like Patricia Cornwell, who worked in the Virginia chief medical examiner's office for six years before writing *Postmortem*, her first novel featuring her creation, medical examiner Dr. Kay Scarpetta.

"The creative, spontaneous soul sends forth its promptings of desire and aspiration in us, These promptings are our true fate, which is our business to fulfill." —D. H. Lawrence

Some writers describe an urgency they experience once they have their idea. Once it exists, the idea seems to insist that it be written. Nora Okja Keller told *Poets and Writers* magazine that she heard a Korean woman named Keum Ja Hwang talk at the University of Hawaii. The woman described how, as a "comfort woman" in the Second World War, she had been raped repeatedly by Japanese soldiers. After hearing this story, Keller had violent nightmares.

"I felt like the only way to exorcise it all from my dreams was just to write it down."

The idea can take the form of a cause. Harriet Beecher Stowe wrote *Uncle Tom's Cabin* propelled by a determination to expose slavery:

"The Carthaginian women in the last peril of their state cut off all their hair for bow-strings to give to the defenders of their country; and such peril and shame as now hangs over this country is worse than Roman slavery, and I hope that every woman who can write will not be silent."

An idea can simply occur to a writer, to her extraordinary good fortune. J. K. Rowling describes how Harry Potter arrived:

"Where the idea for Harry Potter actually came from I really couldn't tell you. I was travelling on a train between Manchester and London and it just popped into my head. I spent four hours thinking about what Hogwarts would be like—the most interesting train journey I've ever taken. By the time I got off at King's Cross [station] many of the characters in the books had already been invented."

Haruki Murakami told *Salon* where he got the idea for his extraordinary novel *The Wind-Up Bird Chronicle*:

"When I started to write, the idea was very small, just an image, not an idea actually. A man who is 30, cooking spaghetti in the kitchen, and the telephone rings—that's it. It's so simple, but I had the feeling that something was happening there."

"What I need to do when I'm writing something is figure out what it is I'm thinking about and where my energy is. And (this time) my energy was in the thought that I couldn't do it. So I decided, OK, that's what I'm going to write about. Then it started to fall into place." —Charlie Kaufman on *Adaptation*

"There are several subjects that are themselves not intrinsically funny—aging, illness and war among them—yet writers like Muriel Spark, Stanley Elkin and Joseph Heller have all discovered their innate potential for dark comedy." —Hilma Wolitzer, *The Company of Writers*

How does inspiration reveal itself? In an introduction to her novel *Frankenstein*, Mary Shelley offers a detailed account of the process of its inspiration. At nineteen, the woman who had "scribbled" as a child and created "castles in the air" in her daydreams visited Switzerland. A party gathered at the home of the poet George Gordon, Lord Byron. It included the-then Mary Godwin; her lover the poet Percy Bysshe Shelley, whom Mary was to later marry; Mary's stepsister (and Byron's lover) Claire Clairmont; and Byron's doctor John Polidori.

During bouts of rain, the group read ghost stories aloud. One night, it was decided to have a competition to create the scariest story. That night, Mary couldn't sleep.

> **"My imagination, unbidden, possessed and guided me, gifting the successive images that arose in my mind with a vividness far beyond the usual bounds of reverie."**

She had a "waking dream," of "the pale student of unhallowed arts kneeling beside the thing he had put together."

> **"Swift as light and as cheering was the idea that broke in upon me. 'I have found it! What terrified me will terrify others; and I need only describe the spectre which haunted my midnight pillow.' On the morrow I announced that I had *thought of a story.* I began that day with the words, *It was a dreary night of November,* making only a transcript of the grim terrors of my waking dream."**

Mary's dream turned into the story that became *Frankenstein*. The immediate inspiration was the ghostly game at the Swiss villa. Academic speculators have found rich material in Mary Godwin's unconventional life as they seek deeper motivations from her life, perhaps the death of her mother after Mary's birth and her own multiple pregnancies. Mary echoed the creative power of her Dr. Victor Frankenstein when she wrote of her book, "I bid my hideous progeny go forth and prosper."

Incidentally, *Frankenstein* was not the only product of the rainy Swiss nights. Dr. Polidori began the "The Vampyre," thus creating another popular fictional genre.

Some claim that getting the inspiration for the idea is actually the easy part. The agent Richard Curtis writes:

> "Ask a professional writer about ideas. . . . In all likelihood, he'll ask, 'Which ideas?,' because he's got a million of them, and his biggest problem is choosing one." —Richard Curtis

> "Ideas are a dime a dozen, frankly. It's what you do with them that makes them worth something. Even the so-called good ones. The U.S. Copyright Office backs me up on this. You cannot copyright an idea; they literally have no value." —Stuart Spencer, *The Playwright's Guidebook*

> "I think writers are hard-wired for stories, it's what we do, it's what we are." —Nora Roberts

We return to the notion of receptivity. As you live your life, look around you. Carry a notebook with you. You might overhear two people in a railway station and catch half a line: What's their story? Or you might find an old newspaper lining a drawer. Start to read, find a story.

> "Writing—true writing—is not the natural by-product of an isolated experience, not the autonomous creation of an isolated man, but the consequence of a collision of the two." —Archibald MacLeish on Ernest Hemingway

I f you're an established writer, you might receive a commission—that is, you might have an idea handed to you, although this doesn't mean you have to be inspired by it:

> "While I was writing *The Way We Live Now,* I was called upon by the proprietors of the *Graphic* for a Christmas story. I feel with regard to literature somewhat as I suppose an upholsterer and undertaker feels when he is called upon to supply a funeral. He has to supply it, however distasteful it may be." — Anthony Trollope

> "The lamest assignment I ever took was to write a piece for *Details* about buying my first suit. The deal was for $2,000 plus a free suit. I wrote the thing and got a suit from Barneys which I still wear. The real bonus, though, was that *Details* never ran the piece." — Jonathan Franzen

"Self—Family—Community—this is the stuff of life. You cannot be a great writer if you're afraid to live. And living a life colored by a unique heritage is truly glorious. *Celebrate your body, soul, and culture.*" —Jewell Parker Rhodes, *Free Within Ourselves*

The well-known tale of where Ann Rule got the idea for her first book is instructive. Rule had studied creative writing at university as well as psychology and criminology and had been a policewoman in Seattle. Armed with all this experience, Rule wrote stories for crime magazines under a male pseudonym, "Andy Stack." Meanwhile, over a period of some years in the mid-1970s, serial killer Ted Bundy murdered at least sixteen women in Washington, Utah, Colorado, and Florida. To her horror, Ann Rule realized that she had worked with Bundy at a crisis hotline in Seattle. For a time, they had been friendly. After Bundy's trial, Rule wrote *The Stranger Beside Me*, a classic of the true crime genre, of which Rule has been a mainstay for more than twenty years.

Clearly, the odds that a crime writer discovers that one of her old acquaintances was really a notorious serial killer are long in the extreme. It is the kind of story that would stretch your credulity if you read it in a novel. What we see here is how important luck can be. An idea can fall fully-formed into someone's lap. The key is your *receptiveness*. When the opportunity presented itself, Ann Rule followed through triumphantly.

READING AND WRITING

"The ugly fact is books are made out of books. The novel depends for its life on the novels that have been written."
—Cormac McCarthy

"I loved books and I wrote some."
—Saul Bellow

In 1968, the French philosopher Roland Barthes pronounced the author dead. In the writer's place came the reader. "A text's unity lies not in its origin but in its destination," he wrote. Yet, despite the best efforts of structuralists, there are still writers and there are still readers, codependents all.

It is the easiest advice and the best advice for someone who wants to write: READ. While you're doing it, it's important to broaden your horizons. And that doesn't mean you have to read the "classics" just because you think you should. You should seek out writers who are new to you, ones you thought you wouldn't like or those you've never heard of. Join a reading group, if you can, because that will ensure you'll read books that someone else recommends. Read interviews with writers you like, or their biography, and see what *they* like to read. Explore genres: Read a thriller or a romance. Ask your friends what they are reading. Sneak a peek at a couple of lines of what the person sitting next to you on the bus is reading. Read a big bestseller and see if you can figure out why it is popular. Read.

> **"Read widely, read enthusiastically, be guided by instinct and not design. For if you read, you need not become a writer; but if you hope to become a writer, you must read."** —Joyce Carol Oates

In his autobiography, Upton Sinclair exuberantly, and self-importantly, describes his discovery of literature during a Christmas holiday he spent in his youth in the home of his Uncle Bland in Baltimore:

> **"I read Shakespeare straight through during that holiday and, though it sounds preposterous, I read all Milton's poetry in those same two weeks. Literature had become a frenzy. I read while I was eating, lying down, sitting, standing, and walking; I read everywhere I went—and I went nowhere except to the park to read on sunshiny days. I averaged fourteen hours a day, and it was a routine matter to read all of Shakespeare's comedies in two or three days, and all his tragedies in the next two or three, and the historical plays over the weekend. In my uncle's library reposed beautiful volumes, untouched except by the hand of the parlormaid; now**

I drew them forth, with love and rapture, and gave them a reason for being. Some poet said to a rich man, "You own the land and I own the landscape." To my kind uncle I said, "You own the books and I own the literature."

"Faulkner's *As I Lay Dying* had an immense effect on me, and most of my novels bear the burn marks of this experience, those short chapters with their conflicting points of view, truth expressed by multiple perspectives." —Peter Carey

"Along in my sixteenth year I had become possessor of a stout, well cramm'd one thousand page octavo volume (I have it yet,) containing Walter Scott's poetry entire—an inexhaustible mine and treasury of poetic forage (especially the endless forests and jungles of notes)—has been so to me for fifty years, and remains so to this day." —Walt Whitman, *A Backward Glance O'er Traveled Roads*

"You can hear Joyce in Dos Passos' *U.S.A.* and Dos Passos' *U.S.A.* in Mailer's *The Naked and the Dead*. Writers teach other writers how to see and hear." —Wallace Stegner

Most writers can rattle off a list of writers and books that have stayed with them:

"I am an obsessed reader of Finnegans Wake—I must have read it at least half a dozen times—and every time I read the Anna Livia Plurabelle section I hear the voices of my mother and my aunts as they walk among the graves in old Iona cemetery and it is getting dark." —Joseph Mitchell

Some writers stop reading when they are involved in composing their own work. Others consciously avoid their own field when they read.

In a letter in 1948, Wallace Stevens corrected his correspondent.

"You are wrong, by the way, in thinking that I read a lot of poetry. I don't read a line."

Stevens felt it was too easy to pick up something, a word or an influence, even inadvertently.

"The problem for any writer in any field is being circumscribed by what has gone before or what is being printed that very day in books and magazines." —Ray Bradbury

"I read [Ulysses] in bits and pieces and fits and starts until I lost all patience. It was premature brashness. Years later, as a docile adult, I set myself the task of reading it again in a serious way, and it not only was the discovery of a genuine world that I never suspected inside me, but it also provided invaluable technical help to me in freeing language and in handling time and structure in my books." —Gabriel García Márquez, *Living to Tell the Tale*

"My own literary heroes and models, the people who made me want to write, were all American: [Anne] Tyler, Lorrie Moore, Tobias Wolff, Carver, Ford, Roth . . . " —Nick Hornby

"For a long time, I never thought I would be a writer, because to me, a writer was a white man with a long beard. But being influenced by the work of Toni Morrison, James Baldwin, Emily Dickinson, Gwendolyn Brooks, and Robert Hayden, as well as [Langston] Hughes, helped me become a writer myself." —Rita Dove

"James Joyce, Ernest Hemingway, F. Scott Fitzgerald, John O'Hara, Raymond Chandler, Dashiell Hammett, James M. Cain, T. H. White." —Ed McBain

"William Golding, Nadine Gordimer, Saul Bellow, Cormac McCarthy, Toni Morrison, Margaret Atwood, Peter Carey and Jim Crace." —Rose Tremain

"I read biography to learn what a man's life might encompass. I read Moss Hart's 'Act One.' I read Arna Bontemps, Langston Hughes, Richard Wright, W. E. B. Du Bois' *The Souls of Black Folk*, I read *Up From Slavery*. I read the Emancipation Proclamation and the Constitution of the United States." — August Wilson

While you are reading, you should retain your critical eye. Don't feel overwhelmed, especially when you read a book as rich, dense, and multi-layered as *Ulysses* or *Gravity's Rainbow*. You have the opportunity to learn from them as you prepare your own work.

"The masters, whose work has justifiably stood up for decades, and rings as true today as the day when it was printed, are not for that reason to be taken as perfect. It is

necessary while learning from them, not to be intimidated, and to remember they didn't tell all the stories, or invariably tell the ones they picked with ultimate, unapproachable skill."
—George V. Higgins

Unusually, Barbara Kingsolver's novel *The Poisonwood Bible* includes a bibliography and an author's note. The novel is set in the Congo in colonial times. The author couldn't visit the perennially unstable country of Zaire, as independent Congo was called in the 1990s, so she relied on her memory and other books, among them Chinua Achebe's *Things Fall Apart*. Thus a direct line can be drawn connecting Achebe's book with Kingsolver's and Joyce Cary's, a link in a vast web that includes everything ever written that was ever read.

GETTING STARTED

"The fact is, it's easier to write than it is to want to write. Just pick up your pen, put down a word. Any word."

—John Dufresne

Each published writer's story of how he or she got started is unique. At some juncture in their lives, the writers whose accounts are included here, and which are included for inspiration, found the time to satisfy their inclination to write. And then, fortuitously, they uncovered their own talent. It is facile to say, but they'd never have known if they hadn't tried. In each case, we might imagine what would have happened had they not made a start when they did. Writing is one of the easier activities to put off till tomorrow. It takes time. The rewards are not immediate. But there comes a moment when you just have to start.

In an interview with *Publishers Weekly*, Nora Roberts describes being marooned by snow at home with her children: "When school was canceled every morning for a week, I'm not ashamed to admit I wept," she says. On impulse, she decided to write down one of the stories in her head. "As soon as I started, I fell for the process of writing, and I knew it was what I should have been doing all along."

Initially, Roberts wrote for herself. "It didn't matter to me whether they got published or not, it was something I needed to do for me." Roberts wrote six manuscripts before she got published, and now she sells more books than any writer in America.

Multiple bestseller writer Mary Higgins Clark worked as a flight attendant for Pan Am, got married, had five children, and was widowed in her thirties. She had always wanted to write and had taken writing courses at New York University. Before she hit pay dirt, Clark worked in radio, getting up at five A.M. to write before getting her kids ready for school.

"I knew I had the talent. When I was fifteen I was picking out clothes that I would wear when I became a successful writer. I was sure I'd make it, but you have to learn the craft, how to tell the story."

At the age of ten, Nobel Prize–winner Nadine Gordimer was unaccountably removed from her school in a small town in South Africa by her mother. She found company in her local library by reading D. H. Lawrence, E. M. Forster, Thucydides, and Proust. The reading turned the young Gordimer to writing. Sixty years later, she recalled the reaction she felt when her first story was published:

"To see this story in print—and they didn't know it had been written by a 15-year-old girl—there's never been a moment like it. I don't think even the Nobel Prize was as thrilling."

Once Michael Connelly decided he wanted to be a mystery writer he took deliberate career steps to furnish himself with the tools of that particular writing trade. Connelly was a sophomore at the University of Florida studying construction when he had his Eureka moment watching Robert Altman's *The Long Goodbye*. Connelly went to the source and read all of Chandler's novels. He decided he wanted to change his degree to a double major in journalism and creative writing, thinking this would take him where he now wanted to go.

Connelly worked the crime beat at various papers in Florida—in 1985, he was a member of an *Orlando Sun-Sentinel* team nominated for a Pulitzer Prize for reporting the crash of Delta Flight 131. He then worked for the *Los Angeles Times*. It was in Los Angeles that Connelly created his peerless detective, LAPD veteran Harry Bosch. Connelly wrote when he wasn't reporting, and on his third attempt, he wrote *The Black Echo*, which the Mystery Writers of America gave their Edgar Allan Poe Award for best first novel.

Many writers don't begin writing straight out of college. Instead, they switch careers later in life.

Eric Jerome Dickey was working in Los Angeles as a software developer for the aerospace company Rockwell by day while doing stand-up in clubs at night and taking acting classes. His first writing was a screenplay, which led to writing classes at city colleges in L.A. After he was laid off by Rockwell, he went to UCLA to study writing. A short story

> Ian Fleming claimed that he wrote *Casino Royale*, the first James Bond book, to take his mind off the fact that he was getting married for the first time at the age of forty-three. Fleming, who was a journalist at the time, wrote the book in 1952 at his place in Jamaica called "Goldeneye." "I didn't read it through as I wrote it," he said. "When I got back to England and did so I was really appalled." But once he was finished, Fleming treated himself to a custom-made gold-plated typewriter.

became *Friends and Lovers*, the first of his highly successful novels.

Best-selling writer W. E. B. Griffin was born William Edmund Butterworth III and has written under eleven pen names in addition to his own. Griffin has a military background. He was working at Fort Rucker, in Alabama, when he spent three weeks writing his first book. Called *Comfort Me with Love*, it sold for $1,000. He was soon matching his $5,000 army salary with each book he sold, so he quit the army to write full time. Griffin's big break came with writing sequels to the first *M*A*S*H* book. Griffin told CNN he made $50,000 for the first sequel, *M*A*S*H Goes to New Orleans*. He wrote a dozen more, and each sold more than 1 million copies, he said.

E. L. Doctorow worked as a reader for a movie company. His first novel, *Welcome to Hard Times*, was inspired by that experience.

> "I had to read one rotten Western after another, and it occurred to me that I could lie about the West in a much more interesting way than any of these people were lying."

Doctorow worked as an editor at the publisher New American Library and was editor-in-chief of the Dial Press until he turned to writing full time after the success of *The Book of Daniel* in 1971.

In the reading group guide to her novel, Julia Glass described how she got started as a novelist, now known for the bestseller *Three Junes*. Glass was working at *Cosmopolitan* as a copyeditor and she tried, and failed, to sell her employer "Souvenirs," a short story she'd written about traveling in Europe. Years later she looked at the story again and decided that the third most important character in the story as written was the most interesting. Glass rewrote the story as "Collies" and it was rejected again. She sold some other stories but resisted working on a novel as agents suggested:

> "When I wrote to a fellow writer how unfair it felt that these agents wouldn't consider story collections, he wrote back something like 'Stop complaining, get off your duff, and just write a novel. If you want to, you can.' I was momentarily hurt, but I knew he was right. Sometimes I wonder if I would ever have written *Three Junes* without that kick in the pants."

◎ ◎ ◎

A writing career can begin at any point in one's life, even without prior writing experience, and any set of circumstances may give rise to it. It's never too late to start.

Few writers, however, start as late as Mary Wesley, who died in 2001 at the age of 90. Wesley received little schooling, married a baron, worked for British intelligence in the Second World War, and had two children. After her second husband died, she needed a means of support.

> **"I had no money except for my widow's pension and £50 a month from some family trust, and no qualifications for work."**

In 1983, Wesley's first novel, *Jumping the Queue,* was published and she wrote prolifically from then on. Her later novels include *The Camomile Lawn* and *A Sensible Life*. Readers commented on the lusty sexiness of her books.

> **"People are startled by my books, because they think 'how can an old woman write about sex?' As though one could forget it . . . The idea that people go on being sexy all their lives is little explored in fiction."**

Barbara Kingsolver's Web site notes that when Kingsolver became pregnant, she suffered from insomnia.

> **"Instead of following her doctor's recommendation to scrub the bathroom tiles with a toothbrush, Kingsolver sat in a closet and began to write *The Bean Trees*, a novel about a young woman who leaves rural Kentucky (accent intact) and finds herself living in urban Tucson."**

John Grisham went to law school at Ole Miss, practiced law for ten years, and served in the Mississippi House of Representatives from 1983 to 1990. At the DeSoto County courthouse, he heard a twelve-year-old's testimony of her rape and was driven to write *A Time to Kill*, his novel of extralegal revenge. Grisham got up at five in the morning to write, taking three years to finish the book, which was published in an edition of 5,000 by Wynwood Press. He sold his second book, *The Firm,* to Paramount and then to the New York publisher Doubleday, after which it spent 47 weeks on the *New York Times* bestseller list, becoming the best-selling novel of 1991.

> "I didn't study writing, I didn't go to writing school, I didn't join any writing groups, I didn't study English literature. It just kind of evolved. I got into the habit of writing notes, and then it would be sketches. It started when I was going across the States in a Greyhound. I was so bored, so I took a little notepad, and started writing things to amuse myself. And then when the whole HIV thing hit Edinburgh, I wanted to write about that in some way." —Irvine Welsh

George Pelecanos told *Book Page* about his wide range of jobs: bartender, truck driver, line cook, valet, and shoe salesman. Pelecanos was general manager of a $30 million company when he had what he calls an "early mid-life crisis" and quit work and wrote *A Firing Offense*. Pelecanos's bravery and confidence can drive all would-be writers.

> "You've got to remember, I was just a guy saying, 'I want to write a book.' I didn't have any formal training. I never took a writing class, so I'm sure the people around me that loved me were thinking, 'He's gonna fail.' And how would they know, and how would I know, that I could write a book? I just thought that I could. I just had the idea that I could."

AUDIENCE

"I don't write for myself. And I don't think a book is an end in itself. A book is just a bridge, that you cross to touch somebody and grab someone by the neck and say, 'Hey I believe this. You want to hear this story? You want to share this with me, this wonderful experience of storytelling?'"

—Isabel Allende

Every writer begins with what E. B. White describes as an audience of one. The writer may never be able to please her first reader, because she can be the most demanding and most relentless of critics.

"Your whole duty as a writer is to please and satisfy yourself, and the true writer always plays to an audience of one. Start sniffing the air, or glancing at the Trend Machine, and you are as good as dead, although you may make a nice living." —E. B. White, *The Elements of Style*

Writers are always ready to essay an opinion of their audience:

"My writing is not of the commercial theatre. When plays of mine succeed in it, it is in spite of all the commercial dogmas which never consider the theatre as a medium for Art." — Eugene O'Neill

"Some portions of the book are powerfully written; but my writings do not, nor ever will, appeal to the broadest class of sympathies, and therefore will not attain a very wide popularity." — Nathaniel Hawthorne on *The Scarlet Letter*

E. B. White is talking about published writers; those who know they have an audience of paying customers who must be enticed back each time they publish. The unpublished writer who aspires to publication has to begin by impressing a couple of people: an editor and whoever controls the purse strings at the publisher or the magazine, or a literary agent who will provide access to them.

The publisher's job is to think about the book's potential audience. In *Thinking Like Your Editor*, Susan Rabiner and Alfred Fortunato say that the publisher will make a decision—whether to offer you a contract and for how much—based on an evaluation of four questions, which are, essentially,

1. Does the book have an audience?
2. Who is in the audience?
3. What will this particular book say to them?
4. Will they want to buy the book?

If the author has a publishing history, the editor will hope the audience (those who bought the last book) will remain loyal and that they can increase that number and "break out." The publisher will also take other factors, such as competition and subject matter, into consideration. They'll hope against hope that a book whose audience at first may seem limited actually "crosses over." The audiences for Lance Armstrong's autobiographical book and for Laura Hillenbrand's *Seabiscuit* have gone way beyond cycling fans and horse-racing aficionados.

If you've never published before, the publisher or editor will make a guess—an educated guess, but a guess nonetheless.

◎ ◎ ◎

Nathaniel Hawthorne never thought his books would "cross over" to a wider audience, but he did test them on his wife. He said *The Scarlet Letter* had a tremendous effect on her. "It broke her heart and sent her to bed with a grievous headache—which I look upon as a triumphant success! Judging from its effect on her and the publisher, I may calculate on what bowlers call a 'ten-strike.'"

Perhaps worried about getting this sort of reaction, Herman Melville warned Sarah Huyler Morewood about *Moby Dick* in a letter:

"Dont you buy it—dont you read it, when it does come out, because it is by no means the sort of book for you. It is not a

piece of fine feminine Spitalfields silk—but it is of the horrible texture of a fabric that should be woven of ships' cables and hawsers. A Polar wind blows through it, & birds of prey hang over it. Warn all gentle fastidious people from so much as peeping into the book—on risk of lumbago & sciatics."

Really, you shouldn't worry about inducing sciatics in readers or how many people are going to like what you've written. Get it down first. Even if no one but you likes what you produce, what you have done is still an achievement. If someone else likes it too, so much the better.

It might be that you are only concerned about the audience of one. Perhaps you are writing a journal for yourself.

"I came eventually and by slow degrees to write *The Lord of the Rings* to satisfy myself: of course without success, at any rate not above 75 percent." —J. R. R. Tolkien

"Today too little is made of all the writing that doesn't seek publication, all the letter writing, e-mail sending, recipe copying, and diary keeping—all the writing that minds our lives. Now there is a great emphasis on turning one's diary into a published memoir or novel, and any number of books will advise you how to do so. But I believe there is still enormous value in the piece of writing that goes no farther than the one person for whom it was intended, that no combination of written words is more eloquent than those exchanged between lovers or friends, or along the pale blue lines of private diaries, where people take communion with themselves." —Betsy Lerner

"Often I ask others, 'Who are we *really* writing for?' A future self, usually. Journal keeping is that rare activity centered in the present, contemplating the past, yet aimed for a future self." —Alexandra Johnson

You might want to write your personal history not only for yourself but also for members of your family.

"A teenager wants to know, did her grandmother love music, did she dance, and to what music? A young sports enthusiast wonders, what games did grandfather play? A beginning cook longs for her mother's recipes, and wonders if mother remembers any of grandmother's recipes or, better yet, wrote them down." —Linda Spence

Tristine Rainer, in *Your Life as Story*, writes about what she calls New Autobiography or personal nonfiction narrative or literary memoir. It is a democratic form, something anyone can write by, about, and for herself or himself:

"No longer does literature have to be written by recognized writers with a body of work. It can be an unpublished book or one autobiographical story by a man who never wrote anything else. Its value may be measured not in how many people it reaches or good reviews it receives, but in the experience creating it gives the writer."

Writers who have written like this and then exposed the results to the world have found wide publishing success in recent years. Rainer cites books like Donna Williams's *Nobody Nowhere*; William Styron's *Darkness Visible*; Elizabeth Wurtzel's *Prozac Nation*, Mark Doty's *Heaven's Coast*, Mikal Gilmore's *Shot in the Heart*, Carolyn See's *Dreaming*, Nathan McCall's *Makes Me Wanna Holler*, Terry Tempest Williams's *Refuge*, and Nancy Mairs's *Ordinary Times*.

Of course, not everyone agrees that it's possible or best for a writer to write without thinking about an audience.

"Liars say they write only for themselves." —Sol Stein

"I write books for readers, I don't write books for myself. They aren't particularly matters of self-expression to me. If I were going to just write to express myself, I think actually I'd find something easier to do." —Richard Ford

In 1978, Isaac Bashevis Singer was awarded the Nobel Prize in Literature. At his banquet speech, Singer commented, with an eye to the adults in his immediate audience and elsewhere,

"Ladies and Gentlemen: There are five hundred reasons why I began to write for children, but to save time I will mention only ten of them. Number 1) Children read books, not reviews. They don't give a hoot about the critics. Number 2) Children don't read to find their identity. Number 3) They don't read to free themselves of guilt, to quench the thirst for rebellion, or to get rid of alienation. Number 4) They have no use for psychology. Number 5) They detest sociology. Number 6) They don't try to understand Kafka or *Finnegans Wake*. Number 7) They still believe in God, the family, angels, devils, witches, goblins, logic, clarity, punctuation, and other

such obsolete stuff. Number 8) They love interesting stories, not commentary, guides, or footnotes. Number 9) When a book is boring, they yawn openly, without any shame or fear of authority. Number 10) They don't expect their beloved writer to redeem humanity. Young as they are, they know that it is not in his power. Only the adults have such childish illusions."

TIME AND SPACE

"Ninety-five percent of everything I've written has been done in bed."

—Paul Bowles

"I walk my dogs in the morning and map out what I'm going to do that day in my head. Then I go home and do it. Very boring process, really."

—Dennis Lehane

When do you write? When the kids have gone to bed or before they get up? Do you write in the middle of the night or at dawn? Do you write before school, after school, or during school? Where do you write? In an office, in a hotel room, in a shed in the woods?

If you're lucky, you can set aside a designated space and some uninterrupted blocks of time. If not, you write when and where you can. J. K. Rowling wrote in Edinburgh coffee houses while her baby napped. The British writer Magnus Mills, whose novel *The Persistence of Beasts* was short-listed for the Booker Prize, worked as a bus driver. Mills wrote down ideas on the back of overtime slips as his bus idled at red lights.

First, *when*.

In *Becoming a Writer,* Dorothea Brande prescribes an exercise: Pick a time and make yourself sit down and write at that time every day. If you miss too many appointments, she says, you can put that time to another use. "*If you fail repeatedly at this exercise, give up writing.*" It takes discipline to spend precious free time in an activity that might seem like hard work, so it makes sense to approach it in a businesslike fashion.

Professional writers make their own hours. How they spend their time away from writing is up to them.

"There is something machine-like about the way Ackroyd lives his life: writing from 7:30 A.M. till 9 P.M., with breaks for household chores and food; drinking from 9 P.M. till sleep. You seem ferociously disciplined about work and drink, I say. 'What else is there?' he says. Is there anything else? 'Not in my life, no.'" —Simon Hattenstone, *The Guardian,* on Peter Ackroyd

"I normally get up around 8 A.M. I eat breakfast, read the newspaper, and read and answer e-mail. I start writing between 10 and 11 A.M. and write five pages per day. I'll then eat a light lunch, take an hour nap, and work on a screenplay in the afternoon." —Robert Parker

Graham Greene was asked about his work day:

Q: "Are you a nine-till-five man?"
A: "Good heavens, I would say I was a nine-till-a-quarter-past-ten man."

Greene also said he set himself a word minimum to write each day. In his younger days it was 500 words, but it later went down to 200. Every writer's daily stamina is different, and you should be aware of your limit. At a certain point— after two solid hours, say—you might find that everything you produce takes three hours to fix.

Next, *where*.

Eugene O'Neill wrote standing up at a tall desk in longhand in tiny script; Edith Wharton in bed.

> "She used a writing board. Her breakfast was brought to her by Gross, the housekeeper, who almost alone was privy to this innocent secret of the bedchamber. (A secretary picked up the pages from the floor for typing.)" —R. W. B. Lewis, *Edith Wharton*

> "All the desks of my life have faced windows and except for an overwrought period in the late 1980s when I worked on a word processor, I have always spent most of my time staring out of the window, noting what is there, daydreaming, or brooding." —Joyce Carol Oates

In an article called "Shedding Writer's Block" in the *Christian Science Monitor*, Noel C. Paul wrote about the popularity of writing sheds, from Thoreau's at Walden Pond onward.

> "When I wrote the following pages, or rather the bulk of them, I lived alone, in the woods, a mile from any neighbor, in a house which I had built myself, on the shore of Walden Pond, in Concord, Massachusetts, and earned my living by

the labor of my hands only. I lived there two years and two months. At present I am a sojourner in civilized life again." — Henry David Thoreau, *Walden*

"In 1906," Paul writes, "Irish playwright George Bernard Shaw built a hut on a rotating platform that he could move to follow the sun's path across the sky." John Cheever, on the other hand, worked in the basement of his building in New York on a card table set before a blank wall.

"You have to put your pants on in the morning and go some-place." —Frank Conroy

At his National Book Foundation Medal Award presentation in 2000, Ray Bradbury described how he wrote *Fahrenheit 451* in the basement of the library at UCLA and how the book came to be published:

"I had no money to rent a proper office. I had a large family at home and I needed to have a place where I could go for a few hours. I was wandering around the UCLA campus and I looked down below and I listened, and down in the basement I heard this typing. So I went down in the basement of the UCLA library and by God there was a room with 12 typewriters in it that you could rent for 10 cents a half-hour. And there were eight or nine students in there working away like crazy, so I moved in there one day with a bag of dimes and I began inserting dimes into the machine and the machine released the typewriter, and you'd have half an hour of fast typing.

Can you imagine what it was like to write *Fahrenheit 451* in the library where you could run upstairs and feel the ambience of your beloved writers; and you could take books off the shelf and discover things that you might want to put in your book as a quote and then run back down and finish writing another page. So over a period of nine days I spent $9.80 and I wrote *Fahrenheit 451*.

"I always write first thing in the morning. If it's really going, I'll start at 4 or 5 o'clock and that will go through till lunchtime. And if it's gone well, I'll have a couple glasses of wine with lunch as a reward. It's like a dog getting his biscuit."—John le Carré, *Entertainment Weekly*

Where you write can have a definite effect on *what* you write.

"It all began during the summer of 1945, in a barn in Waitsfield, Vermont, where I was on sick leave from service in the merchant marine, and with the war's end it continued to preoccupy me in various parts of New York City, including its crowded subways, in a converted 141st Street stable, in a one-room ground floor apartment on St. Nicholas Avenue, and, most unexpectedly, in a suite otherwise occupied by jewelers located on the eighth floor of 608 Fifth Avenue. It was there, thanks to the generosity of Beatrice and Francis Steegmuller, then spending a year abroad, that I discovered that writing could be just as difficult in a fellow writer's elegant office as in a crowded Harlem apartment. There were, however, important differences, some of which worked wonders for my shaky self-confidence and served, perhaps, as a

Walk past any Starbucks coffeehouse and you are likely to see many of the tables occupied by someone working on a laptop. A few of the people will look as though they moved in days before. Places like this can be a refuge for writers, and even if a cup of coffee costs $3.00, you can't buy office space for that.

Alisa Valdes-Rodriguez worked on finishing her novel *The Dirty Girls Social Club* at a Starbucks in Albuquerque. She needed somewhere to write, because with a baby son, she couldn't get anything done at home. She told *Publishers Weekly*,

> **"I was fuelled by white chocolate mocha and cappuccino. The staff thought that I was strange because I was there all the time. I would be there 10 to 15 hours a day for two weeks."**

Valdes-Rodriguez, also a journalist and a musician, went on to receive $500,000 for her novel.

catalyst for the wild mixture of elements that went into the evolving fiction." —Ralph Ellison, *Introduction to the Thirtieth Anniversary Edition of Invisible Man*

In 1928, Edmund Wilson was rewriting his novel *I Thought of Daisy* in Santa Barbara. He wrote to his editor Maxwell Perkins:

"The weather is beautiful and all the days are exactly alike. The calm Pacific spaces are excellent for work. I always feel stamped in New York. But if you stayed out here very long, you would probably cease to write anything, because you would cease to think—it isn't necessary out here and the native regard it as morbid."

"I like the proximity to the industry I work in. It demystifies how contracts happen, how advances are determined, how a review gets assigned, the size of reviews, even the content. Publishing loses that inaccessible, magical quality when you live in New York." —Jonathan Franzen, *New York Magazine*

What you use, whether it's a quill pen dipped in ink, like Shelby Foote, or a Mont Blanc pen; whether you write on an IBM ThinkPad or a note pad, is up to you.

"For thirty glorious, labor-laden days he wrote with his thick pencil on the rough scratch paper, made his few word corrections, and transferred the material to the typewriter. He neglected everything else—friends, family, debts, the new baby, galley proof arriving in daily batches from Macmillan, living only with his dog Buck. . . . " —Irving Stone, *Jack London: Sailor on Horseback*

Thomas Hardy wrote *Far from the Madding Crowd* in and out of Bockhampton in Dorset. "Occasionally without a scrap of paper out the very moment when [I] felt volumes . . . [I] would use large dead leaves, white chips left by the wood-cutters, or pieces of stone or slate that came to hand."

"My main problem in writing this book is that my trusty old Sears electric typewriter, which I used to type out my school reports with one finger, had bitten the dust five years earlier, and being computer illiterate, I had no realistic way to put my story on paper. Except the old-fashioned way. So I hope you can appreciate that what you are about to read was written by hand on 760 pages of notebook paper in seven weeks spanning May 7 to July 1, 1999." —Mick Foley, *Have a Nice Day!*

"She never wrote down a sentence until she clearly under-stood what she wanted to say, had deliberately chosen the words, and arranged them in their right order. Hence it comes that, in the scraps of paper covered with her pencil writing which I have seen, there will occasionally be a sentence scored out, but seldom, if ever, a word or an expression. She wrote on these bits of paper in a minute hand, holding each against a piece of board, such as is used in binding books, for a desk. This plan was necessary for one so short-sighted as she was; and, besides, it enabled her to use pencil and paper, as she sat near the fire in the twilight hours, or if (as was too often the case) she was wakeful for hours in the night. Her finished manuscripts were copied from these pencil scraps, in clear, legible, delicate traced writing, almost as easy to read as print." —Elizabeth Gaskell, *The Life of Charlotte Brontë*

There are extraordinary examples of how creativity can overcome almost any physical obstacle.

In December 1995 Jean-Dominique Bauby, the editor of French *Elle*, was left a quadriplegic by a devastating stroke. Bauby was held prisoner by "locked-in syndrome"; his mind was active, but the only muscle Bauby could move was in his left eyelid. Bauby devised a means of writing that enabled him to laboriously compose his autobiography, *The Diving Bell and the Butterfly*. An assistant would read the letters of the alphabet, reordered with the most common letters first. (In French, the six most common are *E, S, A, R, I,* and *N.*) Bauby would blink his eye when he heard the letter he wanted to use. In this way, over time, Bauby compiled his book, which contrasted the being held captive in a useless body (the diving bell) with the freedom of his spirit (the butterfly). Bauby died a couple of days after the release of the book in France in 1997.

The British astrophysicist Stephen Hawking has suffered from Lou Gehrig's disease—ALS (amyotrophic lateral sclerosis)—for three decades. Hawking has made enormous contributions to our understanding of the universe, and his *A Brief History of Time* was, at 10 million copies, one of the best-selling science books of all time. At one point, he underwent a tracheotomy to help his breathing that made it impossible for him to speak, and he had to communicate much like Jean-Dominique Bauby, choosing letters of the alphabet that were shown to him. But a computer program called E Z Keys allowed Hawking to synthesize speech, and he has adapted the system so that he can give live lectures and write at up to fifteen words a minute by saving the words to disk.

You create an environment you find conducive to work. Robert Caro showed a reporter from the *Columbia Journalism Review* his office in a building in midtown Manhattan. The reporter described the office as "monastic," with only a picture of an empty U.S. Senate chamber on a bulletin board as adornment. (Caro was finishing *The Master of the Senate* at the time.) The desk held only white legal pads, galley pages for his book, and a Smith Corona Electra 210 typewriter of which Caro had bought seventeen when the company took them out of production. The room had a minimum of distractions. "It's too easy not to write," Caro said, "If you could do anything else, you'd be doing it."

FORM

> "I think I am a short story writer naturally. I know I could never write a poem and I never intended to write a novel. Every single one of my novels came about accidentally, that is, I thought I was writing a long story."
>
> —Eudora Welty

You want to write, but to write what, exactly? A memoir; history; poetry; a novel? Or a short story, perhaps. Or a long short story.

While they are theoretically allowed to exercise their free will, many writers will contend that they've been invisibly but firmly propelled in one particular direction. Writers might write what they like to read, and we have heard how reading is the foundation of writing. Following your own reading tastes might help you narrow the field: fiction or nonfiction; poetry or prose. If you love movies, or the theater, or TV, you may be driven to write in those genres.

Short stories are a sensible starting point for a fiction writer. Theoretically, and obviously, a short story shouldn't take as long to write as an entire novel. Theoretically. The scope and scale can remain manageable. Unlike most forms of nonfiction, you don't necessarily have to do any research before you start a story. You can sit down right now and have at it. Once you've finished, there is an established circuit of journals and magazines you can submit your story to.

Certain writers found that the short story suited their writing beautifully: Eudora Welty, John O'Hara, Raymond Carver, Peter Taylor, Flannery O'Connor, John Cheever, Ann Beattie.

> "I did try to write poetry for 10 years. And I've been trying to write a novel for almost 10 years. But neither of those forms have given me the satisfaction of the short story. I think the short story is closest to the joke in a way. It's a quick gift, clears the air, makes you look at your life differently—if just for a minute." —Molly Giles

Edgar Allan Poe found a particular virtue in brevity:

> "If any literary work is too long to be read at one sitting, we must be content to dispense with the immensely important effect derivable from unity of impression—for, if two sittings be required, the affairs of the world interfere, and everything like totality is at once destroyed."

Poe went on to say that no poem should be so long that it can't be read at one sitting. He also saw form as being decided in part by subject:

> "Beauty is the sole legitimate province of the poem . . . Now the object, Truth, or the satisfaction of the intellect, and the object Passion, or the excitement of the heart, are, although attainable to a certain extent in poetry, far more readily attainable in prose."

In an introduction to a book of long short stories published in 1991, Saul Bellow wrote of the short attention span of the modern reader when so many media are competing for our time.

> "It would be mad to edit a novel like *Little Dorrit*. That sea of words *is* a sea, a force of nature. We want it that way, ample, capable of breeding life. When its amplitude tires us we readily forgive it. We wouldn't want it any other way. Yet we respond with approval when Chekhov tells us, 'Odd, I have now a mania for shortness. Whatever I read—my own or other people's works—it all seems to me not short enough.' I find myself emphatically agreeing with this. There is a modern taste for brevity and condensation. Kafka, Beckett, and Borges wrote short. People of course do write long, and write successfully, but to write short is felt by a growing public to be a very good thing—perhaps the best. At once a multitude of possible reasons for this feeling come to mind: This is the end of the millennium. We have heard it all. We have no time. We have more significant fish to fry. We require a wider understanding, new terms, a deeper penetration." —Saul Bellow

Although many writers' first published work is a story, most try to move to the longer form as soon as they've got a few stories under their belt. It is often a commercial consideration. Generally speaking, short stories sell many fewer copies in book form than novels. Publishers would much rather a writer give them a novel than a book of stories. (And they will do almost anything to avoid having to publish a novella, a short novel.)

The transition from short stories to novels can prove difficult, involving as it usually must not just extra length but more breadth and depth too. Norman Mailer describes the process:

"I remember the summer before my Junior year, working on my very first novel, *No Percentage* (which will remain forever unpublished), I ran into a phrase by Henry James. He spoke of 'the keeping up.' That can be the first horror to face when you're young. Your novel tends to change all too quickly. It may even be the cardinal reason why people in college tend to stay away from longer fiction. Young short-story writers, no matter how good, often blow up when they attempt a longer work. They'll have a good beginning but the second chapter goes off and they never get it back. The sad truth is that a would-be novelist has to start a few books that do give out, or even crash before a sense of the difficulties is acquired. If the same likelihood of early failure applied to young race-car drivers, there would not be speedways." — Norman Mailer

"You know, I never had anything against short story writers writing novels, if they wanted to or felt they could, or should. My whole argument was against a short story writer being compelled to write novels when he didn't know how, or wasn't ready." —Katherine Anne Porter

"One sees a lot of novel-length 'fiction' manuscripts that aren't novels and a lot of shorter fiction 'pieces' or 'works' of fiction that aren't short stories. To say 'oh, boy, we've got a whole "new" kind of fiction, the idea of it is *nothing happens*,' is to deny fiction its own meaning. It's like saying, 'we've got this neat new shade of red—*green!*' Why call it fiction at all? Call it something else. 'Green writing,' say. Or 'FAIP,' short for 'Fooling Around in Prose.'" —Rust Hills

It might be that you have a true story that could either be told "straight" as nonfiction or that could be worked into a novel. Henry Miller chose to write autobiographical fiction. In his *Tropic of Cancer*, Miller wrote, "This is not a book. This is a libel, slander, defamation of character . . . ," and so on. Not that Miller was concerned, but these are issues that might not arise in a novel.

A writer can get away with more in a novel than in a work of nonfiction, although autobiographies often blur that particular distinction. And, while nonfiction writers have long been criticized when they invent dialogue or make suppositions, they are basing their writings on factual evidence. (One hopes.) Novelists have more freedom to invent, although they, too, must be wary of writing about characters whose real identity can be recognized.

"In fiction a narrator may be—and often famously is—unreliable (as in *The Good Soldier, The Great Gatsby*, Philip Roth's Zuckerman novels). In non-fiction, never." —Vivian Gornick

"I always wanted to write fiction, from a really early age. After university, I worked in publishing, and then I started writing reviews, and I got a job feature-writing. And actu-

Perhaps we should take our lead from the Russians and not be so concerned about form and genre. Write it and let the Library of Congress, whose job this is, assign it a category.

"In fact, none of the great Russian prose writers of the nineteenth century, with the possible exception of Turgenev, was on easy terms with the novel as genre. Gogol called *Dead Souls*, his only novel-length work, a poem. To define this unusual 'poem' he invented the notion of a hybrid genre, midway between epic and novel, to which he gave the name 'minor epic.'" — Richard Pevear, *Introduction to Anna Karenina*

ally—this sounds like a joke about English journalism—that satisfied a lot of my fictional urges. I mean, I was never a straightforward reporter. I wrote fairly long features that allowed me to have fun." —Zoë Heller

"Write the truth and no one believes you: it's too alarming. So you might as well make it up." —Fay Weldon

Arundhati Roy is one writer who would argue with a distinction between the "true" and the "made-up." She has written the novel *The God of Small Things* and a number of essays and books about, among other things, Indian politics and the global economy.

"I don't see a great difference between *The God of Small Things* and my works of nonfiction. As I keep saying, fiction is truth. I think fiction is the truest thing there ever was." — Arundhati Roy

Occasionally a book will straddle existing forms, or create new ones. In 1966, Truman Capote's *In Cold Blood* took a novelistic approach to an all-to real crime and established a new paradigm, the "nonfiction novel," in Capote's words. Norman Mailer's *The Executioner's Song* is the novelist's account of the life of Gary Gilmore, who, in 1977, was the first person executed in the United States in ten years. The book combines prodigious research and journalism in an account of the life, crimes, and state-sanctioned death of an actual person, yet it is a novel (it won the Pulitzer Prize for fiction in 1980). Mailer has said that book made him realize that "God is a better novelist than the novelists. The story was not only incredible, but it most certainly had happened."

Echoing something William Zinsser says on page 86, Annie Dillard detects in Mailer's choice of form a literary pecking order.

"Mailer's calling this documentary account of the life and death of convict Gary Gilmore a novel seems to say, This text is meaningful, it is a work of art. The cultural assumption is that the novel is the proper home of significance and that nonfiction is mere journalism." —Annie Dillard, *Living by Fiction*

We can only look on enviously when a rare writer like Suzan-Lori Parks disdains to choose and conquers the world in almost every format. Her play *Top Dog/Underdog* won the

2002 Pulitzer Prize for drama, and she has a number of other successful plays under her belt. In 2003, she was working with Oprah Winfrey's production company to develop Toni Morrison's *Paradise* and Zora Neale Hurston's *Their Eyes Were Watching God* for large and small screen and was writing a musical called *Hoopz,* about the Harlem Globetrotters, for Disney. There was a report about her writing a movie for Brad Pitt. Parks had previously written the script for the movie *Girl 6,* directed by Spike Lee. Also in 2003, Parks's novel *Getting Mother's Body* was published.

Parks told the *Atlanta Journal-Constitution* that the theater actually constituted a detour for her when she was a student at Mount Holyoke College. Sometimes there are larger forces at work.

"I was taking a creative writing class with James Baldwin back in college. When it was my turn to read from my short story, I would stand and gesture a lot. He finally said, 'Have you ever thought of writing for the theater?' I was totally not into theater at all, at all, at all. But it was *James Baldwin,* and I did what he said. So I became a playwright."

Labels and Categories

⊙ ⊙ ⊙

"I wrote *Knots and Crosses* not even realising that
I was writing crime fiction. I used to go into bookstores
and I'd take my books off the crime fiction shelves
and put them in with Scottish literary fiction."

—Ian Rankin

"I began to write in 1931, at the age of eleven.
I did not try to write science fiction, but tackled
something much more primitive."

—Isaac Asimov

Academics make careers out of describing who was influenced by whom and how. Together with critics, they collect writers into schools, camps, trends, and tendencies. Writers of a similar age are also liable to be called a "generation," even if they have little in common. And publishers put writers in categories and attach labels like "literary" (which can mean difficult or pretentious), or "popular" (which can be used as a pejorative by literary snobs).

Many published writers work hard to shed labels. Others find it difficult to switch from one category in which they have become established into another. Unlike his phenomenally successful courtroom thrillers, John Grisham's *A Painted House* contained no lawyers at all, but Grisham's fans stuck with him.

The aspiring writer should be aware of the likelihood of getting labeled, although it is certainly not a pressing concern. A reader at a publishing house may comment that your manuscript reminded him or her of X. Even if you haven't read X or don't know who X is, "like X" will be attached to the manuscript if it gets to move around the house.

You might actively want to embrace a category. Popular fiction, especially paperback fiction, is divided into a number of quite strictly defined categories like science fiction, fantasy, and, biggest of all, romance. As we'll see, some of these categories have rules you'd better learn if you want to succeed.

First, the iniquities of the label.

"When men write about 'ordinary people,' they are thought to be subtle and sensitive. When women do, their novels are classified as domestic." —Carol Shields

Ernest Gaines was interviewed by Jeanie Blake for the *Xavier Review*:

Q: "You've been labeled a black writer, a Southern writer, a Louisiana writer, a California writer. Which are you?"

A: "I don't care what the hell people call me. I just don't give a damn. By the time they start categorizing me I'm thinking about something else to write about."

Two words you wouldn't want associated with your work are "junk" and "bad," but John Gardner and Virginia Woolf make them almost sound like compliments:

"Not everyone is capable of writing junk fiction: It requires an authentic junk mind. Most creative-writing teachers have had the experience of occasionally helping to produce, by accident, a pornographer. The most elegant techniques in the world, filtered through a junk mind, become elegant junk techniques." —John Gardner, *The Art of Fiction*

"My real delight in reviewing is to say nasty things; and hitherto I have had to [be] respectful. The worst of it is, I find, that very few people have the brains to write a really *bad* novel; whereas anyone can turn out a respectable dull one." —Virginia Woolf

If you actively seek out a niche, you might find the field to be clearer. James Glieck described how he started as a science writer for the *New York Times Magazine*.

"As a kid on the metro desk I couldn't go to them and say, 'I'd like to write a big piece about Middle Eastern politics'; they had plenty of people who knew about that. But I *could* go to them and say, 'I want to write about this new thing called chaos theory,' and they would say, 'Okay.'" —James Glieck in *Publishers Weekly*

The fantasy genre is one of the most popular on the fiction shelf. The popularity, even the existence, of fantasy has been ascribed to the work of J. R. R. Tolkien. Terry Brooks for one has said that when he read *The Lord of the Rings*, he found what he was looking for.

"I think the so-called 'fairy story' one of the highest forms of literature, and quite erroneously associated with children (as such)." —J. R. R. Tolkien

In one particularly useful passage on SciFi.com, Terry Brooks breaks down the difference between science fiction and fantasy and adds a helpful line about mystery writing too.

> "The readership for fantasy is four-to-one than science fiction—maybe larger than that. That is due to the fact that fantasy is a much more accessible form of literature. You don't have to have any pre-existing knowledge to get into a fantasy; you kind of feel that you do with science fiction because it has all that science in there.
>
> "There is an off-putting element to science fiction, unfortunately, that deters a lot of people from picking it up. Where everybody was raised on fairy tales, legends and myths—and so they can leap on into that.
>
> "It is also the reason that mysteries are so popular. It's not because they are all that wonderful, they are so easy to get into. It takes no effort to read one." —Terry Brooks

Isaac Asimov would be undeterred by "all that science":

> "My books tend to celebrate the triumph of technology rather than its disaster. This is true of other science fiction writers as well, notably Robert Heinlein and Arthur Clarke. It seems odd, perhaps significant, that the Big Three are all technological optimists."

In 1992, the Science Fiction Writers of America became the Science Fiction and Fantasy Writers of America, recognizing the kinship of the emerging genre of fantasy. Greg Bear has written about the categorization they can both suffer:

"All my life I have tried to explain the difference between writing imaginative literature—science fiction and fantasy—and writing contemporary fiction. My explanations usually fail. There is no real difference, there is only class distinction, distortions caused by historical trauma and literary snobbery (science fiction is the literature of 'tradesmen,' not 'gentlemen')."

Occupying a realm in the same galaxy as science fiction is speculative fiction or alternate history, concerned with the great "What ifs": What if Hitler had won the Second World War or the South had won Gettysburg? One of the major figures in this field is Harry Turtledove, who describes how his fellow writer Judith Tarr got him to thinking:

"Judy was complaining one day that the cover art on an upcoming novel of hers was 'as anachronistic as Robert E. Lee holding an Uzi.' I looked at that line in her letter and I thought 'I can do something with that.' And when I wrote her back I asked, 'Who would want to give Robert E. Lee an Uzi? Time traveling South Africans, maybe? If I write it, I'll give you an acknowledgment.'"

"I don't read much horror, though I like the *idea* of horror, the idea of a nasty, subversive genre, the purpose of which is to upend conventional ideas of good taste, and to speak truths otherwise ignored or suppressed. I think that's really worthy." —Peter Straub

The largest category in all of fiction is romance. Those who aspire to writing romances will undoubtedly be helped by the

Romance Writers of America (RWA), whose Web site is packed with information about romantic fiction. The RWA provides figures that prove the popularity of the genre. In 2001, romance generated $1.52 billion, representing 54.5% of paperback sales. Romance had 51.1 million readers in 2002

The romance category accounts for 36% of the market in popular fiction and is sub-divided into genres and even sub-genres. They are:

Contemporary romance—romances set after the World Wars

Historical romance—romances set before the World Wars

Inspirational romance—romances containing spiritual themes

Paranormal romance—romances containing 'other-worldly' elements such as magic, mystic characters, or fantasy and science fiction elements and Time-travel romance—(Included in our Paranormal sub-genre) romances set in two different time periods, with characters "time-traveling" between both.

Regency romance—romances set in England in the early 1800s

Romantic suspense—romances containing mystery and intrigue.

and owned almost 36% of the market share of popular fiction. (This is versus 27% for mystery/thriller, 17% for general fiction, 7% for science fiction, and 14% for the unlikely "other" grouping of "religious, occult, male adventure, movie tie-in.")

Romance, clearly, is big business. The RWA has 8,400 members. More than 2,000 romances were published by major houses in the United States in 2001, so if publication is your be-all and end-all, you might like these odds better than trying to write *Catch-22* for the twenty-first century.

The RWA also helps by spelling out exactly what a romance must have to be called a romance: "Two basic elements comprise every romance novel: a central love story and an emotionally satisfying and optimistic ending." No ifs, ands, or buts: There has to be a love story at the core of the book and the ending *has* to be happy. No bittersweet twists or hard-luck stories and certainly no outright tragedies. As long as the novel satisfies these criteria, you're good to go.

Having this helpful advice and a roadmap from the RWA doesn't mean writing romances is easy. There is more opportunity, but there is also more competition, and it is difficult to stand out in a crowd.

Mystery has its own conventions, such as the distinction between the amateur sleuth and the professional (there's less procedure for the amateur), and which breaks down still further from "hard-boiled" writers beginning with Dashiell Hammett to writers of "cozies," in which all the crime takes place off-page.

The Mystery Writers of America performs a service for the mystery community similar to that of the RWA for romance writers. There is also Sisters in Crime, "an international organization of writers, readers, booksellers, librarians, agents, editors, reviewers and teachers interested in promoting the work of women mystery writers," which provides guidance, support, and information. Sisters in Crime has 3,200 members, more than 900 of whom are published mystery writers.

For writers of every category there is the Author's Guild, which offers advice on every aspect of the business from how to negotiate a contract to help with setting up your own Web site. (I have to mention the guild-maintained www.ianjackman. com.) The guild also acts as a pressure group for writers, advocating for their behalf on matters like fair compensation, free expression, and copyright protection.

There are more categories, of course. Espionage, which struggled with the end of the Cold War, but survived it, and suspense. But it is really only important to focus on excellence. Some writers simply transcend any genre, and defy the categorization they may be subjected to. This reader would identify as genre transcenders Michael Connelly, John Le Carré, P. D. James, Ruth Rendell, Ian Rankin, Raymond Chandler, Dennis Lehane, and Eric Ambler, among others. Ultimately, the only category or label that is really significant is "good." If you write well enough, you'll find your place on the shelf.

GRAMMAR AND OTHER NUTS AND BOLTS

◎ ◎ ◎

"A preschooler's tacit knowledge of grammar is more sophisticated than the thickest style manual."
—Steven Pinker, *The Language Instinct*

"What you need to do is get hold of *The Elements of Style* by Strunk and White, and more or less memorize it."
—Ursula K. Le Guin

Kurt Vonnegut's novel *Bluebeard* purports to be the autobiography of Abstract Expressionist painter Rabo Karabekian, whose pictures are Mark Rothkoesque monoliths of color with names like *Windsor Blue Number Seventeen*. Because he became famous by applying large amounts of paint in uniform blocks, many of the people in Karabekian's life didn't think he could actually draw. But Karabekian has a secret locked up in a potato barn on his property, a secret he reveals at the end of his autobiography as a huge super-real painting he has made. The painting is eight feet high and sixty-four feet long and is populated with tiny renderings of more than fifty-two hundred people from the artist's life. "The picture was so realistic," Karabekian tells us, "that it might have been a photograph." This Abstract Expressionist could actually paint. He was a brilliant draughtsman all along.

In a similar way, if you want to be playful with words and manipulate them thoroughly, you need to be sure how they are properly applied. In order to abandon the rules, you have to know what the rules are, and you can't ignore them if you don't know them. Most adventures in grammar are just mistakes, and the great experimenters, like Gertrude Stein or Samuel Beckett, certainly knew what they were doing when they set about dismantling English as we know it.

Learning grammar can only help with your writing. Seeing how sentences are constructed in classically correct form forces you to think about your method and ensures that you'll look hard at every line you write. Good grammar also inspires confidence in a reader. Perhaps it is more accurate to say that nothing dissipates a reader's goodwill like an easily avoided grammatical clunker.

No one should despair—help is available. If you didn't take Ursula Le Guin's advice about *The Elements of Style*, you can always look up something that you're uncertain about. (That or which? Semicolon or comma?)

If it comes to it, and you are published, your work will be looked at by copyeditors, who are gifted individuals with an encyclopedic knowledge of grammar *and* access to grammar manuals for good measure. They are the driver's mechanic. A copyeditor is likely to change some of what you write. Publishers have different house styles, and many follow guides like *The Chicago Manual of Style* and *Words into Type*. Is *Presi-*

dent always spelled with a capital *P?* (No.) Does everyone use the serial comma? (No.)

> "*Whom* turns up in odd places because it is supposed by some to be a nicer, classier, word than *who*, just as *I* is often thought to outrank *me* (between you and *I*), but the supposition is groundless. These are all just words, which belong in some places at some times and not in others at other times." — Thomas Parrish, *The Grouchy Grammarian*

> "My printers always inform me that I know nothing of punctuation and I give thanks that I have no responsibility for any of its absurdities." —Wallace Stevens

Not all writers are as grateful as Stevens. In a story in the *Guardian*, Brian Whitaker wrote about T. E. Lawrence and his refusal to spell Arabic names with any consistency in his work. (Transliteration is another subjective area.) In 1926, a proofreader pointed out that Lawrence's *Revolt in the Desert* was riddled with inconsistencies. The city of Jeddah was as often as not spelled "Jidda." A man named Sherif Abd el Mayin in the first instance was also el Main, el Mayein, el Muein, el Mayin, and le Muyein. Lawrence replied that Arabic itself was not uniform and didn't lend itself to exact replication.

> "There are some 'scientific systems' of transliteration, helpful to people who know enough Arabic not to need helping, but a washout for the world," he said. "I spell my names anyhow, to show what rot the systems are."

Writing on the Internet often has its own grammar and punctuation. The e-mail is gradually replacing the hand-written letter. E-mails and, to an even greater extent, text messages are often composed in a kind of coded shorthand, the effect of which is bound to creep into the broader language over time.

"The truth is that much of what passes for writing in cyberspace is dreadful. The spelling in e-mail is rotten, the grammar is atrocious, the punctuation—don't ask. And e-mail isn't the half of it. Some of the drivel in chat rooms and instant messages, on bulletin boards and Web pages doesn't deserve to be called writing." — Patricia T. O'Conner and Stuart Kellerman, *You Send Mail*

We come to the writers who have ignored the conventions of grammar or followed their own. George Bernard Shaw was exasperated with the English language and made up his own alphabet. William Faulkner was something of a grammatical pioneer:

"Faulkner was in some ways an extremely consistent writer. He never included apostrophes in the words 'dont', 'wont', 'aint', 'cant', or 'oclock', and very seldom used an apostrophe to indicate a dropped letter in a spoken dialect word, such as 'bout' or 'runnin'. He never used a period after the titles 'Mr', 'Mrs', or 'Dr'. The editors of the first editions generally, but

inconsistently, accepted these practices, but compositors often made mistakes, and many periods and apostrophes slipped in." —Joseph Blotner and Noel Polk, *Introduction to William Faulker: Novels 1942–1954*

Blotner and Polk give examples of some of the numerous editorial changes and mistakes that were made in Faulkner's work. The title *If I Forget Thee, Jerusalem* was changed to *The Wild Palms*. In *Requiem for a Nun*, Faulkner wrote about "Juneteenth," the day of the black celebration of the ending of slavery. An editor erroneously changed it to "June Tenth."

"When I first began writing, I felt that writing should go on, I still do feel that it should go on but when I first began writing I was completely possessed by the necessity that writing should go on and if writing should go on what had colons and semi-colons to do with it, what had commas to do with it, what had periods to do with it what had small letters and capitals to do with it to do with writing going on which was at that time the most propound need I had in connection with writing." —*Gertrude Stein*

In this spirit, Samuel Beckett's *How It Is* originally had no punctuation at all and was intended to run uninterrupted in three pieces of prose. Beckett eventually split the words into more digestible chunks two to six lines in length.

So while it's true that the first thing no one will ever say of an aspiring writer's work is, "Her grammar is wonderful," a piece with even a couple of artless solecisms is asking to be rejected out of hand. In and of itself, grammar might be less important than style or concrete techniques like plot and character, but contributes significantly toward the first impression your work will give. And grammar is one of the few parts of writing that can definitely be learned as arduous a task as that might be .

The best custodians of the language rejoice in the changeability and constant evolution of the whole shebang, including the grammatical conventions.

"The English language is a dreadful mess. It always has been and always will be. That is its great splendour." —Matthew Parris, *introduction to The King's English by H. W. and F. G. Fowler.*

Style

"Young writers often suppose that style is a garnish
for the meat of prose, a sauce by which a dull dish is made
palatable. Style has no such separate entity;
it is nondetachable, unfilterable."
—E. B. White

"Omit needless words."
—Strunk and White

All writers have a style, or styles. When writing about
style, writers will commonly say that they started out
trying to write like someone they liked to read. Then they
developed their own style and their own voice emerged organ-
ically.

"There are two kinds of writers. Faulkner, Fitzgerald, and
Hemingway, Melville and James, write with an air that is
inimitable. There are other writers, usually less famous, who
go along in a variety of modes. I'm in the latter camp."
—Norman Mailer

Your style should be liberating. If you are too self-conscious, that will probably show:

> "In *The Deer Park* I had been trying to find a style through three drafts. The first had been Proustian—not first-rate Proust, of course. Attempted Proust. Failed Proust. The second draft was located somewhere between the English novel of manners and Scott Fitzgerald—not good, but in that general direction. Then I found a tone that was not like the others. It fit the essential material. So I learned how style literally repels certain kinds of experience and can be equal to a dominating wife who is ever ready to select you suits. If a writer insists on a specific tone, despite all inner warnings, it can even limit the varieties of experience that will enter the book." —Norman Mailer

The watchword to style is *clarity*. Your style shouldn't be stylized or forced. As you're developing a narrative or telling a story, don't get in your own way. Less *is* more.

> "Writing is devilish; the general sin is wordiness." —Sheridan Baker

> "A style interests when it carries the reader along: it is then a good style. A style ceases to interest when by reason of disjointed sentences, over-used words, monotonous or jog-trot cadences, it fatigues the reader's mind. Too startling words, however apt, *too* just images, too great displays of cleverness are apt in the long run to be as fatiguing as the most over-used words or the most jog-trot cadences." —Ford Madox Ford

"[Hemingway] understood . . . that what the writer knows but omits will show up in what he writes as a sense of unstated depth that is more powerful than any attempt to describe the undescribable can be. Good prose, Hemingway insisted again and again, must be like an iceberg, seven-eighths submerged; like dynamite packed under a bridge. . . . " —Ann Douglas, *Terrible Honesty*

When reading about style, Hemingway's name always comes up, usually as an exemplar of fine style. George V. Higgins says that Hemingway "for all practical purposes formed the American Style for this century." Higgins's advice: "If you wish to learn how to write, read Hemingway."

Can you consciously adapt someone else's style? Can you learn style?

"The search for style is a fool's errand: You have it, whatever it is, from the day you put the first word on a page." —Michael Seidman

You can try to learn style, or, more accurately, how to change and improve the style you already have. Look at the writer whose style you liked and try to see how he or she does it: short, choppy sentences or long, elaborate, subordinate-clause marathons. Look at your own sentences and notice your tendencies. Read E. B. White's essay in Strunk and White and look at Elmore Leonard's "Rules of Writing" on his Web site. From "Never open a book with weather," to "Keep your exclamation points under control," they are a fount of good sense. Leonard advises, for example, that you use only "said" to carry dialogue. "I once noticed Mary McCarthy ending a

line of dialogue with 'she asseverated,' and had to stop reading to get the dictionary."

◉ ◉ ◉

"Good sentences are the sinew of style." —*The Oxford Essential
Guide to Writing*

"A good writer is one you can read without breaking a
sweat." —Patricia T. O'Conner

"Look at your sentences one at a time. Do they appear clean
and seemly, with a regular subject, verb, and direct object? *Do
they make sense?* That's more important than the most eloquent and lyrical embroidery." —Carolyn See

A good place to look at sharp and well-ordered sentences is
newspapers and magazines, where information has to be
imparted in a strictly limited space. Jefferson D. Bates extols
Reader's Digest, which for years has had a feature on vocab-
ulary and can be looked to as a model:

"And while it's long been a popular sport among the literary
intelligentsia to put down the *Digest*, I'll unhesitatingly take
the other side. If you want to find examples of clear, tightly-
edited prose, you'll look a long way to hunt down anything
better than you can encounter in any issue of the much-
maligned *Reader's Digest*."

The Mentor looks to *Sports Illustrated* and *Entertainment
Weekly* for weekly examples of precise and intelligent writing

with all the fat drained out. The inventive and playful pages of *Variety*, where "percenters" (agents) place "thesps" (actors) in "laffers" (comedies) are another source of good, clean fun on the page.

> "We must constantly ask if our words are meaning what they say, and saying what we mean." —Sheridan Baker

> "When writing with maximum impact, the writer seems under compulsion to set down an unbearable accuracy." — Marianne Moore

> "The writer must deal with clichés not by trying to avoid them altogether, but by being aware of their proper use. Tired as they may be, they remain part of the language, and sometimes their employment is more economical than the detours around them. At times, a cliché will serve better than a quasi-original phrase that fails." —*Words Into Type*

The key phrase here is "being aware."

> "It's too easy to fall back on stereotypes and myths, and I think that's what most writers do about Indians and what most men do when they write about women." —Sherman Alexie

> "I notice that you use plain, simple language, short words and brief sentences. That is the way to write English—it is the modern way and the best way. Stick to it; don't let fluff and flowers and verbosity creep in. When you catch an adjective, kill it. No, I don't mean utterly, but kill most of them—then the rest will be valuable. They weaken when they are close

As you seek clarity, you can watch out for signs that you are trying too hard: foreign words; slang in the wrong places; overelaboration. *Words into Type* has five pages of "Trite Expressions," which begin:

Abject apology
Abreast of the times
Accidents will happen
Acid test
Active consideration
Add insult to injury
Adds a note of
After all has been said and done
Age before beauty
Agree to disagree

together. They give strength when they are wide apart. An adjective habit, or a wordy, diffuse, flowery habit, once fastened upon a person, is as hard to get rid of as any other vice." —Mark Twain

"Writing, however, isn't a special language that belongs to English teachers and a few other sensitive souls who have a 'gift for words.' Writing is thinking on paper. Anyone who thinks clearly should be able to write clearly—about any subject at all." —William Zinsser, *Writing to Learn*

"But how does one go about writing clearly? I don't know. I presume you have to start with an orderly mind and a knack for marshaling your thoughts so you know exactly what you want to say. Beyond that, I am helpless." —Isaac Asimov

"I am not pleased when people tell me I have a nice style. It suggests that style is something applied. It is not. Style in itself has no value. I just try to write as clearly as I can to let those thoughts appear on the page. I don't want the style to stand out, I don't want the words to get in the way." —V. S. Naipaul

At the same as you are reading what you've written to check for clarity and meaning, you should *listen* to your writing. Listen to the rhythm, to the cadence—the flow of the words.

"I never wrote a word that I didn't hear as I read." —Eudora Welty

"In both writing and reading, the ear as well as the eye will be at work. We do not only place words on a page, we also hear them, the sense, the cadence, and the emotional vibrations. All our senses must be stirred by our unique and creative susceptibilities: words, written or spoken, do reverberate in the mind." —Hallie Burnett

"Sensory details are critical to powerful writing because they can set a mood; evoke a huge array of feelings; trigger memories for both your character or your readers; and draw them into *believing* that they are right there, in that scene, in that moment, inside your character's mind." —Caroline Joy Adams

"Rhythm is as important a part of a well-written sentence as grammatical correctness. Notice how short and simple sentences can be changed in the following suggested variations.

'He had made her acquaintance. It was amiable. She was a purveyor of ambrosias. She was lying asprawl. She was on a divan. It was a divan of a curious Persian design.'

'He had made the amiable acquaintance of a purveyor of ambrosias who was lying asprawl a divan of a curious Persian design.'" —Karen Elizabeth Gordon, *The Transitive Vampire*

"I learnt a lot of my style from [Hemingway], but he had no sense of humor, so I had to look elsewhere for that." —Elmore Leonard

Plot and Character

> "*Only* trouble is interesting."
> —Janet Burroway

> "Unless something has gone disastrously wrong, other people aren't that interesting to write about."
> —Margaret Atwood

There seems to be general agreement amongst those who write about the writing of fiction that you should concentrate more on crafting satisfying three-dimensional characters than obsessing about the intricacies of the plot (except, that is, in mysteries).

> "Plot is, I think, the good writer's last resort and the dullard's first choice." —Stephen King

> "Plot grows out of character. If you focus on who the people in your story are, if you sit and write about two people you

know and are getting to know better day by day, something is bound to happen." —Anne Lamott

If you hold with what Stephen King and Anne Lamott say, you will concentrate on character first.

"The chief reason for almost any reader to go on turning the pages of almost any novel is to find out what happens next. The reason the reader *cares* what happens next is because of the author's skill at characterization. . . .

It was the ability to create characters readers could care about, too, that made Charles Dickens a monumental popular success. While Oscar Wilde might have remarked that only a man with a heart of stone could read of the death of Little Nell without laughing, the truth of the matter is that readers did not laugh when they read that scene. They wept." —Lawrence Block, *Writing the Novel*

"I must admit that each time I reread the novel, I tend to cry whenever Esther Summerson cries, and I don't think I am being sentimental. The reader must identify with her or simply not read the book in the old-fashioned sense of reading, which is the only sense that matters." —Harold Bloom [on *Bleak House*], *The Western Canon*

Simplistically put, the plot is what happens to the characters—they are what the book is "about."

"The situation comes first. The characters—always flat and unfeatured, to begin with—come next. Once these things are fixed in my mind, I begin to narrate." —Stephen King

"As a rough principle I always begin with one character and then perhaps two, and they seem to be in conflict with each other. 'The cat sat on the mat' is not a story. 'The cat sat on the dog's mat' *is* a story." —John le Carré

"The 'stories' were made rather to provide a world for the language than the reverse. To me a name comes first and the story follows." —J. R. R. Tolkien

Mark Haddon's novel *The Curious Incident of the Dog in the Night-Time* begins with a situation: the description of a dead dog pinned to the ground by a garden fork. The scene is narrated by Christopher, a fifteen-year-old, with a distinctive voice. Haddon told Powells.com:

"The dog came along first, then the voice. Only after a few pages did I really start to ask, *Who does the voice belong to?* So Christopher came along, in fact, after the book had already got underway."

Haddon had worked with autistic children, and Christopher has traits that can be associated with the autistic spectrum, although the word *autism* never appears in the book and, according to *Newsweek*, Haddon would have preferred if the jacket copy hadn't mentioned it either.

Elizabeth Bowen describes the process whereby characters and action come together in a well-crafted story.

"One cannot 'make' characters, only marionettes. The manipulated movement of the marionette is not the 'action'

necessary for plot. Characterless action is not action at all, in the plot sense. It is the indivisibility of the act from the actor, and the inevitability of *that* act on the part of *that* actor, that gives action verisimilitude. Without that, action is without force or reason. Forceless, reasonless action disrupts plot. The term 'creation of character' (or characters) is misleading. Characters pre-exist. They are *found*. They reveal themselves slowly to the novelist's perception—as might fellow travelers seated opposite one in a very dimly-lit railway carriage."
—Elizabeth Bowen

The story's credibility often depends upon how well the author develops the characters, or, following Elizabeth Bowen, how clearly they reveal themselves to the writer.

"The authority of the writer always overcomes the skepticism of the reader. If you know what you're talking about, or if you feel that you do, the reader will believe you. That's why we believe Frank Baum. Who would believe Dorothy and a house and a dog up in a tornado? We believe it because the author believes it. We believe Peter Rabbit because Beatrix Potter believes it. You have to." —Nikki Giovanni

It is one of the most profound of all creative challenges to bring a figure to life using only words on a page. You may have a particular person or people in mind when you do, but still, the character is yours to make.

"The characters you create in a novel become as real in your mind as movie stars." —Norman Mailer

Often a writer, especially in mysteries, will use a character he or she has prepared already. If they are well-enough drawn, with foibles and weaknesses and tics we get to love, we're happy to see them again and again: characters like Philip Marlowe and Harry Bosch, Spenser and Rebus, or Stephanie Plumb and Kinsey Millhone, whom Sue Grafton has guided as of this writing all the way from *A Is for Alibi* through *Q Is for Quarry*.

Once they are released into the world, characters are public figures in some ways. Readers become attached, and they can get upset if a writer treats his creation harshly.

Sir Arthur Conan Doyle created one of the most popular of all fictional characters in Sherlock Holmes, who was introduced along with his sidekick Dr. Watson in "A Study in Scarlet," published in *Beeton's Christmas Annual* in 1887. After a few years, Conan Doyle decided to get rid of Holmes so he could concentrate on the historical fiction he much preferred to write. So, in 1893, in "The Final Problem," Conan Doyle pushed Holmes and his chief foe, Professor Moriarty, over the Reichenbach Falls. Immediately the *Strand* magazine, which was carrying the stories, lost 20,000 subscribers. Conan Doyle was eventually forced to bring Holmes back from the dead, in *The Hound of the Baskervilles* in 1901.

> "When I hear a writer talking earnestly of how the character in his latest book 'took over the action' I am inclined to laugh. . . . Fictional characters are made of words, not flesh; they do not have free will, they do not exercise volition. They are easily born, and as easily killed off." —John Banville

No character is safe. The novelist Pat Conroy was picked by Margaret Mitchell's estate to write a sequel to *Gone with the Wind,* although the projected book never happened. Conroy said at the time that had he written the book, he might have killed off Scarlett O'Hara while she was still beautiful, and we can only wonder what the reaction would have been had that come to pass.

◎ ◎ ◎

You do have to describe your characters to some extent. How much is up to you (Robert Parker won't divulge his Spenser's first name.) You fill in a little of their lives and surroundings.

> **"For a writer, constructing the background material can be so much fun that it's mistaken for writing."** —Ansen Dibell, *Plot*

In some genres, the world you create is a character, too, and Dibell cites fantasy writers who set up their lands and empires over hundreds of pages.

In addition to providing description, you are allowed to digress and diverge, but eventually, unless you are Samuel Beckett or an experimentalist, *something* has to happen. You can still be a minimalist in this regard, like Nicholson Baker, who celebrates the routine and ordinary in his novels *The Mezzanine, Room Temperature,* and *A Box of Matches* and who uses narrative almost in place of plot.

> **"The plot has to be very tiny for me to pay any attention to it for some reason. As soon as my narrators focus on something, they seem to lose track of the fact that they're supposed to be part of some momentous chain of events."**
> —Nicholson Baker

"Very tiny," notice, which does still exist. No matter how small the increments and how expanded each second might be (in Baker's *The Fermata*, for instance), the reader still senses movement.

Plot movement is how you develop your characters, by giving them something to do, and preferably something problematic.

> **"Character is conflict. That is probably said in every writing classroom in the world. Your protagonist is defined by how he faces and overcomes the conflicts in the path ahead."** — Michael Connelly

> **"Don't ask who your character is; ask what your character does."** —Monica Wood

> **"Amiability is the enemy of a story."** —Barnaby Conrad

If you look at any number of famous and popular books, the plot is often surprisingly simple or even, at first glance, banal.

> **"You don't have to be a plot *genius* like Elmore Leonard or Rose Tremain. You don't have to build a state-of-the-art submarine. A sturdy rowboat, even a wooden coat hanger will do you fine."** —Carolyn See

> **"Contrary to what many popular books would like you to believe, there is no formula to assure a great or 'classic' plot. There are no steps, paths, no things you must do, no things you cannot do."** —Noah Lukeman

In the mystery world, in books like the police procedural novel, however, the plot is paramount. A mystery has to be resolved or a killer found. We relish the writer's ability to surprise us with twists and turns—that's why we like these books. The satisfying mystery is the well-constructed book that maintains plausibility. This reader gives demerits when a writer parachutes in a character we've never met as a suspect at the end of the book or when a character gets help from a friend (we've never met him either) who happens to have a specific and obscure technical skill.

If you want to write a mystery, you might start by taking what you've enjoyed and deconstructing it. Strip it down and see how the writer moved from the set up to the conclusion. Figure out how he mixed the red herrings with the real leads and how he teased and tantalized you.

"The first rule of mystery writing can be stated simply: The plot is everything." — Jeremiah Healy

"I think all writing is the same. Suspense, surprise, mystery, impresses in every good writer. The great distinction is that crime writing preserves the idea of a plot." — John Mortimer, *The Paris Review*

"It's a curious fact that if you take a roomful of crime writers and ask them the difference between story and plot, an embarrassingly high number of them will mutter that they really aren't sure." — Lesley Grant Adamson

However much plotting you map out and however many index cards you've stuck to the wall, you'll be on a trip with any number of destinations once you've set off. A lot of the enjoyment in reading is in the excitement of discovery, and it can be in the writing too:

> "My methods of writing might drive a more logical person mad. But it often happens—even with writers who have seen their books clearly from start to finish before they begin— that the book changes itself three-quarters of the way through. This can be the result of a character's not behaving the way you foresaw, a situation that can be good or bad. I do not subscribe to the belief that having a vigorous character who acts for himself is always good. After all, you are the boss, and you don't want your characters running around all over the place, or possibly standing still, no matter how strong they may be.
>
> "A recalcitrant character may veer the plot in a better direction than you had thought at the outset. Or he or she may have to be curbed, changed, or scrapped and rewritten entirely. Such a snag is worth a few days' pondering, and usually requires it. If the character is very stubborn and also interesting, you may have a different book from the one you set out to write, maybe a better book, maybe just as good, but different. You should not be thrown by this experience. No book, and possibly no painting, is ever exactly like the first dream of it." —Patricia Highsmith

TELLING THE STORY

> "'And now the old story has begun to write itself over there,' said Carl [Linstrum] softly. 'Isn't it queer: there are only two or three human stories, and they go on repeating themselves as fiercely as if they had never happened before; like the larks in this country, that have been singing the same five notes over for thousands of years.'"
>
> —Willa Cather, *O Pioneers!*

The object of most of your writing is to tell a story, whether it's fictional or not. The story will have a beginning, a middle, and an end, and in telling the story, you are moving the reader along, maintaining interest and attention from page to page. To facilitate this, the writer has at her disposal an array of devices—species of writing like narrative, exposition, dialogue, background. Each stage of the process: the opening, the second and the third acts, and the ending, has its own particular challenges. When you decide on a point of view, for example, you may be predetermining much of the future of your book in ways you can only imagine at the time.

Each of these is the subject of chapters and, sometimes, whole books in the library of studies and guides. You might want to concentrate your time and resources on one area, such as dialogue, you find particularly troubling.

The literature of the methods of writing is extensive, but the successful assembly of a satisfying whole remains a largely mysterious process.

Before you can begin, you must decide *how* to begin. Do you want to write an outline first? Outlines can become huge and monstrous, but some writers find them essential.

"Some writers never use an outline. Others would be uncomfortable writing anything more ambitious than a shopping list without outlining it first." —Lawrence Block, *Writing the Novel*

"Having written down what it was you intended to do and where it was intended to go can be a big help. Five months after you've started a book, you can still look at the blueprint and know what it was you wanted to accomplish when you started out—not only with the story at large, but with every major plot point and character." —Terry Brooks

"I don't have my novel outlined and I have to write to discover what I am doing. Like the old lady, I don't know so well what I think until I see what I say; then I have to say it over again." —Flannery O'Connor

"With nonfiction, the task is very straightforward: Do the research, tell the story." —Laura Hillenbrand

Edgar Allan Poe would have you know exactly where you are going before you start. His frame of reference is mainly short fiction and the poem.

> "Nothing is more clear than that every plot, worth the name, must be elaborated to its *dénouement* before anything be attempted with the pen. It is only with the *dénouement* constantly in view that we can give a plot its indispensable air of consequence, or causation, by making the incidents, and especially the tone at all points, tend to the development of the intention."

If you are writing longer pieces than Poe tended to do, and you haven't outlined, you'll be marching boldly forward into the dark. Nadine Gordimer starts without notes:

> "I know the end, but—how shall I put it? Other things accrete around the central idea."

Before you get into the body of the piece, you also need to establish a point or points of view.

> "So what is point of view? Most simply stated, it's how the novel is written. That's all there is to it. How the book is written." —Sherri Szeman

> "I'll discuss point of view for a time now. I am beginning to agree with Stegner, that it truly is the most important problem in writing." —Ken Kesey

Patricia Highsmith said she found first person singular most difficult to maintain and third person easier.

"There is another reason why I use the first person. I want to be in the pub myself." —Graham Swift

As for *how many* points of view,

"I prefer two points of view in a novel, but I don't always have them. . . . Using two points of view—as I did in *Strangers on a Train*, the two young men protagonists who are so different, and in *The Blunderer*, Walter and Kimmel, again vastly different people—can bring a very entertaining change of pace and mood." —Patricia Highsmith

"I'm a little shy about telling anyone to go read Tolstoy's *War and Peace*, since it's quite an undertaking; but it is a wonderful book. And from the technical aspect, it's almost miraculous in the way it shifts imperceptibly from the author's voice to the point of view of a character, speaking with perfect simplicity in the inner voice of a man, a woman, even a hunting dog, and then back to the thoughts of the author . . . till by the end you feel you have lived many lives: which is perhaps the greatest gift a novel can give." —Ursula K. Le Guin

The editor Max Perkins would give a copy of *War and Peace* to his writers.

◎ ◎ ◎

Obviously, you must pay close attention to how you open your story. It sets the tone for everything to come.

"The opening lines of a story are a contract with the reader to finish telling the story that is begun." —John Dufresne

"I prefer commencing with the consideration of an *effect*. Keeping originality *always* in view—for he is false to himself who ventures to dispense with so obvious and so easily attainable a source of interest—I say to myself, in the first place, 'Of the innumerable effects, or impressions, of which the heart, the intellect, or (more generally) the soul is susceptible, what one shall I, on the present occasion, select?" —Edgar Allan Poe

"I was sick—sick unto death with that long agony; and when they at length unbound me, and I was permitted to sit, I felt that my senses were leaving me." The opening of Poe's *The Pit and the Pendulum*

A great deal of the doing is in the preparation. Finally, though, you can begin. The best-known opening? The first line of *Anna Karenina*: "All happy families are alike; each unhappy family is unhappy in its own way."

Quiet, loud, tantalizing, obscure, dull: There is no rule. In nonfiction, you can start right at the start:

"I was born in Tuckahoe, near Hillsborough, and about twelve miles from Easton, in Talbot county, Maryland. I have no accurate knowledge of my age, never having seen any authentic record containing it. By far the larger part of the slaves know as little of their ages as horses know of theirs, and it is the wish of most masters to keep their slaves thus ignorant." —*Narrative of the Life of Frederick Douglass, An American Slave*

Or you can describe a set piece, an incident that foreshadows what is to come. In fiction this works too, and takes the form

P resented below are several more notable openings to great novels:

"The *Nellie*, a cruising yawl, swung to her anchor without a flutter of the sails, and was at rest." — Joseph Conrad, *Heart of Darkness*

"In the spring of that year an epidemic of rabies broke out in Ether County, Georgia." — Pete Dexter, *Paris Trout*

"For a long time I would go to bed early." —Marcel Proust, *Swann's Way*

"You better not never tell nobody but God. It'd kill your mammy" —Alice Walker, *The Color Purple*

"It was love at first sight.
    The first time Yossarian saw the chaplain he fell madly in love with him." —Joseph Heller, *Catch-22*

"A screaming comes across the sky." — Thomas Pynchon, *Gravity's Rainbow*

"It was Sunday, and, according to his custom on that day, McTeague took his dinner at two in the afternoon at the car conductors' coffee-joint on Polk Street." — Frank Norris, *McTeague*

"A Frenchman named Chamfort, who should have known better, once said that chance was a nickname for Providence." — Eric Ambler, *A Coffin for Dimitrios*

of coming in during the middle of a scene. Richard Ben Cramer starts his biography of Joe DiMaggio not at Yankee Stadium but on a San Francisco playground with DiMaggio at fifteen. The prologue to Simon Schama's *Citizens*, about the French Revolution, starts forty years after the revolution:

> "Between 1814 and 1846 a plaster elephant stood on the site of the Bastille. For much of this time it presented a sorry spectacle."

> "Joe Gould was an odd and penniless and unemployable little man who came to the city in 1916 and ducked and dodged and held on as hard as he could for over thirty-five years." — Joseph Mitchell, *Joe Gould's Secret*

Once you have started you need to find momentum and keep the story moving with narrative.

> "Narrative should flow as flows the brook down through the hills and the leafy woodlands, its course changed by every boulder it comes across and by every grass-clad gravelly spur that projects into its path; its surface broken, but its course not stayed by rocks and gravel on the bottom in the shoal places; a brook that never goes straight for a minute, but goes and goes briskly, sometimes ungrammatically, and sometimes fetching a horseshoe three-quarters of a mile around, and at the end of the circuit flowing within a yard of the path it traversed an hour before, but always going and always following at least one law, always loyal to that law, which *has no law*. Nothing to do but make the trip; the how of it is not important, so that the trip is made." —Mark Twain

Twain is describing an organic process. Often the patterns and shapes in a book are apparent only once you have reached the end and you see how the book's elements ebb and flow and hold together. This means that you might feel comfortable pressing on, allowing yourself to establish beachheads, knowing you can go back later to trim or add where you need. Richard Preston thanks his editor Sharon DeLano in his credits to *The Hot Zone*. "At one point, I said to her, 'God is in the details,' and she replied, 'No, God is in the structure.'"

"There's an old adage in writing: Don't tell, but show. What does this actually mean? It means don't tell us about anger (or any of those big words like honesty, truth, hate, love, sorrow, life, justice, etc.); show us what made you angry. We will read it and feel angry." —Natalie Goldberg, *Writing Down the Bones*

"Let's say you have broken the ice jam. Your words now pour forth on the page. What words? What words do you write with?

Here is my short answer: the simplest possible words.

Below is my long answer. . . . " —Bill Stott, *Write to the Point*

"If you are stuck at page eighty-seven in your novel, I can't tell you what to write next; nobody can." —Bonni Goldberg, *Room to Write*

"In my editing business, one of the most common weaknesses I see in the middle of a writer's work is disorganization—of sentences, paragraphs, and sections." —Elizabeth Lyon

"*Midpoint* is the center of the book. *Midpoint* is the fulcrum of Act Two. For most writers, Act Two is the tricky trouble-spot, the place where things go wrong. In the heat of creation, you might be tempted to zoom past midpoint. Stop. Slam on the brakes. Slow down." —Robert J. Ray and Jack Remick, *The Weekend Novelist Writes a Mystery*

"It's really deliberate in this one [*Lullaby*] because several readers told me they were disappointed in *Choke* because there was no road trip. The road trip is the perfect second act. Get people together, put them on the road, get them off the road. It's a perfect dynamic montage of scenes." —Chuck Palahniuk

"The joke has it: remembering you set out to drain the swamp is hard when you're up to your ass in alligators. And that is the problem of the second act." —David Mamet

Dialogue is, in most fiction, absolutely essential and is traditionally seen as one of the most difficult devices to pull off convincingly.

"Dialogue is *the* way to nail character, so you have to work on getting the voice right." —Anne Lamott

"Good dialogue moves the plot forward. If you have a scene showing that Brenda and Joe squabble over nothing, and then another scene showing the same thing, the story feels static. It might be true to life, but readers think, What's the point here? You already told me that." —Jerome Stern

"One of the best tests of dialogue is to read it aloud or, even better, have someone unfamiliar with it do the reading. Does it sound like someone speaking, or does it sound like an author trying to create 'realism'?" —Michael Seidman

You can also read other people's dialogue and apply the same test. Take a passage from a writer you like and parse it:

"All right, young woman," said Ken. "Your name."
　"Gloria Swanson."
　"Don't get fresh here. I said your name."
　"Mary Smith."
　"Mary Smith, huh," said Ken. "Age?"
　"Twenty," said Mary Smith. The others laughed.
　"You must have had a hard life," said Ken. "Occupation?"
　"Manicurist," said Mary Smith.
　"She really is, too," said one of the other women.
　"I didn't ask you," said Ken. "Address?"
　"Bellyvue Stratford Hotel, Philadelphia. Bellyvue. Get it?"
The men and women laughed.
　"Ever been arrested before?"
　"Never," said Mary Smith, and the women laughed.
　"How many times you been arrested before, Mary Smith?"
said Ken.
　"I don't know. I didn't keep a diary." —John O'Hara, "Ninety Minutes Away"

O'Hara was not immune to any of the difficulties that can vex a writer midstream. In 1934, the publisher Harcourt Brace paid O'Hara a wage of $50 a week for two months while he finished his novel *Appointment in Samarra*. O'Hara wrote to his brother,

> "But now that it is half finished I am suffering from what Dorothy Parker says Ernest Hemingway calls 'the artist's reward'—in other words, I think what I've written stinks, and I just can't seem to get going again."

All of the perils that have been described, and the various tricks and devices that exist to overcome them, are part of the game the writer plays with the reader. A book, especially a work of fiction, works to convey truth when we all know we are being told a story.

> "Details are what persuade us that someone is telling the truth—a fact that every liar knows instinctively and too well." —Francine Prose

> "It is the responsibility of the writer to put his experience as a being into work that refines it and that makes of it an essence that a wide audience can somehow manage to feel in themselves: 'This is true.'" —Tennessee Williams

You should always try to remember where you are headed, which is toward a conclusion, an ending.

> "You cannot ... promise apples and deliver oranges. The middle of your story—how you've developed the initial promise—determines your ending." —Nancy Kress

It is important to reiterate that you can find help with all aspects of this process. There are books about writing about sex, another difficult matter.

Two of Elizabeth's Benedict's top ten rules for writing about sex are:

1. A sex scene or description is not a sex manual.

5. Sex is nice but character is destiny. —Elizabeth Benedict, *The Joy of Writing Sex*

The editors of the London *Literary Review* bestow an annual award for Bad Sex in Fiction. In 2002, Wendy Perriam, nominated three times in a row, won the tenth award for her book *Tread Softly* and a passage about "erotic pin-striped nakedness." In 2001, Sean Thomas won the award for a passage in which he likened a woman's body to a Sony Walkman.

"If you are writing without moving toward an ending, you are probably just piling up information and—it's all but a dead certainty—being a bore." —Stephen Koch

"When you write happy endings you are not taken seriously as a writer." —Carol Shields

"You should aim for an effect similar to that of the final bars of a symphony. Hearing those, you as a listener know that this is the conclusion, that the work is finished." —H. R. F. Keating

"Yossarian jumped. Nately's whore was hiding just outside the door. The knife came down, missing him by inches, and he took off." —Joseph Heller, *Catch-22*

Occasionally, writers will describe a writing experience as if the writing had guided them rather than the other way round, as if the telling of the story was a truly mysterious and automatic process:

"I am still not able to tell if the novel is all right or absolute drivel. To me, it was written just as if I had sat on one side of a wall and the paper was on the other and my hand with the pen thrust through the wall and writing not only on invisible paper but in pitch darkness too, so that I could not even know if the pen still wrote on paper or not." —John O'Hara

"The writer should be very detached from his work. I've always used the comparison that a writer should be as detached as a heart surgeon is from his work. To write well, you can't be crying as you're cutting someone's heart out." — Ernest Gaines

"Sometime I read [*Caramelo*] over and laugh out loud; I forget I wrote it. More and more, I feel that I'm just channeling, that I'm the instrument, not the music." —Sandra Cisneros

"Sometimes it seems to me that I'm operating myself by remote control from a broom closet in the Empire State Building, but I guess I really am here." —Frank O'Hara

There remains the question of a title. Titles are almost infinitely mutable and they can emerge long after the book itself is done. In *Now All We Need Is a Title,* André Bernard lists titles that some of the most popular books in history might have had if they had not been retitled before publication.

The Salinas Valley	*East of Eden*
Three Tenant Farmers	*Let Us Now Praise Famous Men*
A Silence in the Water	*Jaws*
Pansy	*Gone with the Wind*
The Last Man in Europe	*1984*

REWRITING

"One set of words was the truthful mirror of her thoughts; no others, however apparently identical in meaning, would do."
—Elizabeth Gaskell, *The Life of Charlotte Brontë*

"I'm afraid I've muffed the story,
but I can't do anything about it now."
—John O'Hara on finishing *Appointment in Samarra*

egion are the stories of writers laboring again and again over words and phrases and rewriting endlessly. There are no rules governing the unglamorous work of rewriting, other than the fact that it is necessary and everyone does it. Rewriting is the literary equivalent of sausage-making. You know it goes on, but you'd rather not have to watch. Poe, again, put it well.

"Most writers—poets in especial—prefer having it understood that they compose by a species of fine frenzy—an ecstatic intuition—and would positively shudder at letting the public take a peep behind the scenes, at the elaborate and vacillating crudities of thought—at the true purposes seized only at the last moment—at the innumerable glimpses of idea that arrived not at the maturity of full view—at the fully-matured fancies discarded in despair as unmanageable—at the cautious selections and rejections—at the painful erasures and interpolations—in a word, at the wheels and pinions—the tackle for scene-shifting—the step-ladders, and demon-traps—the cock's feathers, the red paint and the black patches, which, in ninety-nine cases out of a hundred, constitute the properties of the literary *histrio.*"

"It took me six years to finish [*Legs*]. I wrote it eight times and seven times it was no good. Six times it was especially no good. The seventh time out it was pretty good, though it was way too long. My son was six years old and so was my novel and they were both the same height." —William Kennedy

"Many of my shortest and seemingly simple poems took years to get right. I tinker with most of my poems even after publication. I expect to be revising in my coffin as it is being lowered into the ground." —Charles Simic

Rarely does a writer declare herself completely satisfied with what she has written. For the unpublished writer with no externally imposed deadline, the reworking can go on ad infinitum. You might imagine when you are working that you are dealing with two distinct entities—your draft and a polished, beautiful, perfect version of it somewhere out there in the ether. It's your job to reach out and, through your hard work, make your way to it. At a certain point, you have to stop and take stock. With all your rewriting, are you making your manuscript appreciably better? There is almost nothing that can't be improved, but there are many manuscripts that are surely spoiled by too much tinkering and others that are always beyond help. You might be liberated from an unmanageable manuscript if you can set it aside and try something new.

A second opinion can be a great help, provided that the reader promises to be honest. If you read your beloved's novel and you think it's execrable but you say you kinda like it, shame on you. Similarly, you need to be judicious when you ask for help:

> "To lead a disciplined writing life, one must be as free as possible from all 'committee' opinions. Trying to write in a context of external judgments, conflict, hostility, and interruption is incredibly damaging to creativity." —Pat Schneider

> "Caro Mio:
> MUCH improved
> Compliments, you bitch. I am wracked by the seven jealousies. . . . . ." —Ezra Pound to T. S. Eliot on a revision of *The Waste Land*

Writers with a book contract have a deadline: their delivery date. That means they have a target. And even after they have submitted their work to the publisher, and the editing process has seen the manuscript go back and forth, many writers will tinker with the copyedited manuscript and then the typeset page proofs and then the "blues" (the last stage of production), until the very last minute and even beyond the last minute when the book is with the printer and ready to go. This is where a good editor can be invaluable in providing a reality check.

According to his translator Francis Steegmuller, Flaubert created continuity problems for himself with his constant reworking. A doctor's fee might be 100 francs in one version and 75 in another, but the fee was still paid in two-franc pieces, which doesn't work. In another case, a character might sometimes turn left to get to the cemetery from the town square in Yonville, and sometimes turn right.

Other rewriters: Eugene O'Neill wrote seven drafts of *Days Without End*. When Isaac Babel showed his friend Konstantin Pavstovsky a manuscript of 200 pages, Pavstovsky asked Babel if it was a novel. Babel replied that it was 22 versions of his short story "Lyubka the Cossac." Neil Simon also wrote 22 complete versions of his first play, "Come Blow Your Horn," which was in rewrites more than twice as long as it took to write in the first place.

> **"The *Little Foxes* was the most difficult play I ever wrote. I was clumsy in the first drafts, putting in and taking out characters, ornamenting, decorating, growing more and more weary as the versions of scenes and then acts and then three whole plays had to be thrown away."** —Lillian Hellman

Each writer develops her or his own rewriting procedures:

> **"Once something is down I don't usually change it. I do my rewriting every day. I don't rush to the end as I know some writers do, sort of get the whole story down, and then go back."** —Alice McDermott

"When I finish a section, I rewrite that section and then I type that section, and in the process of typing, I cut and rewrite. Then I make penciled changes in the typed copy and give that typed copy to a typist.

"The chapter about Derek, where Slocum loses control, that was four and a half hand-written pages. The next day I started an insert and then wrote an insert in the insert and ended up with 600 pages in that chapter. I used lots of that section later, in other chapters. In fact, when I finished writing that, I knew I could finish the book." —Joseph Heller on *Something Happened*

After a book has been published, a writer may not be able to see it as much more than an interrupted work-in-progress. In later years, the author might have a different perspective on his or her own work. The writer can criticize him or herself from the safe distance afforded by reputation. He or she might acknowledge that the world has moved on in the meantime too. Aldous Huxley wrote *Brave New World* in 1932. In 1946, he provided a foreword to a new edition of his novel:

"Chronic remorse, as all the moralists are agreed, is a most undesirable sentiment. . . . To pore over the literary short-comings of twenty years ago, to attempt to patch a faulty work into the perfection it missed at its first execution, to spend one's middle age in trying to mend the artistic sins committed and bequeathed by that different person who was oneself in youth—all this is surely vain and futile. And that is why this new *Brave New World* is the same as the old one. Its defects as a work of art are considerable; but in order to correct them I should have to rewrite the book—and in the

A writer can pay a lot of attention to the destiny of a single sentence. In the introduction to 1998 edition of *The World According to Garp,* John Irving wrote:

> "Among my many other attempts to begin the novel, I had long ago begun with what would become the last sentence ('... in the world according to Garp we are all terminal cases'), and I recalled how that sentence had moved through the book; I kept pushing it ahead. It was once the first sentence of the second chapter; later it was the last sentence of the tenth chapter, and so on, until it became the end of the novel—the only possible ending. Not surprisingly, Garp describes a novelist as 'a doctor who sees only terminal cases.'"

process of rewriting, as an older, other person, I should probably get rid not only of some of the faults of the story, but also of such merits as it originally possessed. And so, resisting the temptation to wallow in artistic remorse, I prefer to leave both well and ill alone and to think about something else."

Between the first writing of *Brave New World* and the publication of the 1946 foreword, the Second World War had intervened. Many parts of the world were ravaged in ways that would have seemed unimaginable even in 1932, and the atomic era introduced the specter of global war on an even larger scale. Huxley said that in 1932, his Utopia was set 600 years in the future, but by 1946 he thought "the horror may be upon us within a single century."

John Fowles wrote a foreword to a 1978 edition of *The Magus* in which he described some amendments to the original book.

> "The story appeared in 1965, after two other books, but in every way except that of mere publishing date, it is a first novel. I began writing it in the early 1950s, and both narrative and mood went through countless transformations. In its original form there was a clear supernatural element—an attempt at something along the lines of Henry James's masterpiece, *The Turn of the Screw*. But I had no coherent idea of where I was going, in life as in the book. A more objective side of me did not then believe I should ever become a publishable writer; a subjective one could not abandon the myth it was trying, clumsily and laboriously, to bring into the world; and my strongest memory is of constantly having to abandon drafts because of an inability to describe what I wanted."

Twenty years on, in the introduction to the 1998 edition of *The Magus*, Fowles offered another perspective. A writer can reread his own work as well as rewrite it.

> "The book's success has always been something of a puzzle. I can see it is far from being universally well written. I fell into almost every trap awaiting the tyro writer. Yet something in it has evidently called, perhaps especially to the younger. Its very imperfections, its really not knowing quite where it is going, explains in part why it works. Most young people know they don't know; and the not knowing in this

ephemeral, uncertain world is generally the nearest we shall ever get to the truth."

"I used to say that a good writer throws out all the stuff that everybody else keeps. But an even better test occurs to me: perhaps a good writer keeps the stuff that everybody else throws out." —David Mamet

PRODUCTIVITY

> "Some people only have one book in them.
> There are worse things."
>
> —Richard Ford, *The Sportswriter*

> "That, in the writing of books, quantity without quality
> is a vice and a misfortune, has been too manifestly settled
> to leave a doubt on such a matter."
>
> —Anthony Trollope

Some of the greatest American novels of the twentieth century were written by novelists who can hardly be described as prolific. Ralph Ellison (*Invisible Man*) published only one novel in his lifetime. Henry Roth went a full sixty years between the publication of his masterpiece, *Call It Sleep* (1934), and his next novel, *Mercy of a Rude Stream* (1994). The authors of *The Catcher in the Rye* and *To Kill a Mockingbird* may write, but they don't publish.

This last is an important distinction. A few renowned writers are content to write for themselves. For example, the last piece that J. D. Salinger published was "Hapworth 16, 1924" in the *New Yorker* in 1965. There is a difference from what we previously said about an audience of one. Writers such as Salinger found spectacular early success, yet apparently decided they no longer cared to share their work with the world at large.

> "Overpraise tends to lead writers into overproduction. 'Well, I'm so great—why don't I turn out a book a year?'" —Donna Tartt (ten years between *The Secret History* and *The Little Friend*).

It is important to establish your own definition of success. Is it one story? A completed manuscript? One appreciative reader? Publication? A bestseller? A number-one bestseller? Ten number-one bestsellers? Each of these is harder than the last, but none of them is remotely as difficult as capturing something as extraordinary as any of the four renowned novels mentioned in the first paragraph.

Some writers do manage to combine quality with quantity; others merely write a lot of books. But some writers can offer insight into how they accumulate words at pace; others into the slowness with which they have to work. Aspiring writers can find comfort in the latter and, perhaps, marvel that some manage to work so fast.

> "I'll just write until I can't write anymore. If my next book was my last book, I wouldn't care at all. If my next book was my two hundredth from last, it wouldn't bother me. You can only write so long as you feel you've got something to say. I don't think there's any particular virtue in being a writer." — Irvine Welsh

Jack Kerouac could be fast. He was said to have written *The Subterraneans* in three days, and *On the Road* seemed to come quickly to him too. Kerouac's biographer Ann Charters writes that after *On the Road* was published, Kerouac would propagate the notion that he'd written it in three weeks in 1951 on a 120-foot long roll of teletype paper.

Truman Capote famously said of Kerouac, "That's not writing, that's *type*writing." Despite Kerouac's interest in spontaneous writing and his claims of speed, *On the Road* took him a long time to complete. Kerouac began the book in November 1948 and worked on it at a rate of about 1,500 words a day but gave up. The book was revised substantially after the heroic bout with the teletype paper and was finally published in 1957.

(In 2001, Jim Irsay, owner of the Indianapolis Colts football team, bought the Kerouac scroll at auction for $2.43 million.)

In his autobiography, Anthony Trollope described how he would methodically figure out how much he had to write each day to fulfill a publisher's commission.

"When I have commenced a new book, I have always prepared a diary, divided into weeks, and carried it on for the period which I have allowed myself for the completion of the work. In this I have entered, day by day, the number of pages I have written, so that if at any time I have slipped into idleness for a day or two, the record of that idleness has been there, staring me in the face, and demanding of me increased

labour, so that the deficiency might be supplied. According to the circumstances of the time,—whether my other business might be then heavy or light, or whether the book which I was writing was or was not wanted with speed,—I have allotted myself so many pages a week. The average number has been about 40. It has been placed as low as 20, and has risen to 112. And as a page is an ambiguous term, my page has been made to contain 250 words; and as words, if not watched, will have a tendency to straggle, I have had every word counted as I went. In the bargains I have made with publishers I have,—not, of course with their knowledge, but in my own mind,—undertaken always to supply them with so many words, and I have never put a book out of hand short of the number by a single word. I may also say that the excess has been very small. I have prided myself especially in completing it within the proposed time,—and I have always done so. There has ever been the record before me, and a week passed with an insufficient number of pages has been a blister to my eye, and a month so disgraced would have been a sorrow to my heart."

Trollope exemplifies the businesslike approach of professional writers, many of whom habitually keep note of how many words or pages they write in a day. Writing was a job to Trollope. In fact, and almost incredibly, Trollope had *another* job, in the postal service, for much of his writing career.

In his autobiography, Mark Twain echoes Trollope's matter-of-factness:

"I wrote the rest of *The Innocents Abroad* in sixty days and I could have added a fortnight's labor with the pen and gotten along without the letters altogether. I was very young in those days, exceedingly young, marvelously young, younger than I am now, younger than I shall ever be again, by hundreds of years. I worked every night from eleven or twelve until broad daylight in the morning, and as I did 200,000 words in the sixty days, the average was more than 3,000 words a day—nothing for Sir Walter Scott, nothing for Louis Stevenson, nothing for plenty of other people, but quite handsome for me. In 1897, when we were living in Tedworth Square, London, and I was writing the book called *Following the Equator*, my average was 1,800 words a day; here in Florence (1904) my average seems to be 1,400 words per sitting of four or five hours."

Twain and Trollope were both prolific. Neither was as prolific as the most popular writer in America today, Nora Roberts, who has written 69 *New York Times* bestsellers (and probably more by the time you read this.) Roberts has 145 million books in print.

In *I, Asimov*, Isaac Asimov describes having to answer for his productivity.

"All writers have problems. In my case, the most amusing is that of handling people who don't or can't believe I am so prolific. After all, I don't make a point of it. I don't say to anyone, 'Fine weather we're having, and by the way I've published umpty-ump books.'

"But it does come up sometimes. Back in 1979, the first volume of my autobiography had just appeared, and, as it happened, it was my 200th book. I was at a cocktail party or something of the sort and someone who didn't know me and hadn't heard of me (there are billion of such people, unfortunately) said to me, 'What do you do?'

'I write,' I said, this being my standard answer.

I expected him to ask me what I wrote, but he didn't. He said, 'Who is your publisher?'

I said, 'I have a number of publishers, but Doubleday is the most important of them. They have done three-eighths of my books.'

He chose to interpret that remark as a way of aggrandizing myself. Up went his eyebrows, sneer went to his lips, and he said, 'I suppose by that remark you mean that you have written eight books and that Doubleday has published three.'

'No,' I said quietly. "It means I have written two hundred books and Doubleday has published seventy-five.'

At which those people round the table who did know me smiled, and my questioner looked suitably silly."

At the moment he thought up his *Comédie Humaine* in 1833, Balzac is reported to have told his sister, "Salute me for at this very moment I am in the throes of becoming a genius." His series of novels depicting French society ran to ninety-two volumes, five or more of which he might be working on at any one time. Balzac started writing at midnight and sustained himself through the night on strong black coffee.

Perhaps the most prolific writer of all was the English novel factory Barbara Cartland, who holds that honor in the *Guinness Book of World Records*. She was said to have written 723 books and could churn out a novel in either one or two weeks, depending on which account to believe. (Cartland stretches the boundaries of the term *writing*, however, because she dictated her books to secretaries who wrote them up.)

When he was profiled in *Life* magazine in 1958, Georges Simenon was described as the "World's Most Prolific Novelist." Simenon, creator of the Maigret detective series and author of some 400 books, sounded in his profile more like a boxer than a writer. He wrote a novel in eleven days because he said his body couldn't take the strain any longer than that. He insisted on having a physical before he started writing and would take unspecified "pills" when working.

Unless they are writing an opinion piece or an off-the-top-of-the-head memoir, nonfiction writers face an additional requirement that must come before they can write and that can limit the number of books they can complete: the research. (Of course, a lot of novelists also conduct research, but it's not a requirement.) Jonathan Harr spent eight and a half years writing *A Civil Action,* partly because the events he was describing were unfolding as he was working. Eventually he amassed 27 linear feet of research material, much of it from the court cases surrounding the lawsuit over children's deaths from toxic waste in Woburn, Massachusetts, that were at the center of the book. "I regretted getting into this thing more times than I can tell you," Harr said when the book was published. He said a friend told him, " 'Don't do this book. You'll be digging out quarters from behind the car seat.' And he was right."

Robert Caro left his job as a newspaper reporter in New York to write a biography of city developer Robert Moses. He thought the project would take a year, and it took seven. *The Power Broker* (1974) was followed by Caro's *The Years of Lyndon Johnson,* which were researched in heroic depth by Caro and his wife, Ina. The first volume was published in 1982, the second in 1990, and the third in 2002.

As James Thurber and E. B. White once asked, is sex necessary? Two writers with opposite views on what "makeing love," as Hemingway has it, does for literary productivity:

> "If I began to write better it was for two reasons: in my thirties I found my contemporaries and fell happily and deeply in love. There is, I am sure, a direct connection between passionate love and the firing of the creative power of the mind . . . The mind of the restrained or sexually discontented man wanders off into shallows."
> — V. S. Pritchett, *Midnight Oil*

> "I have had to ease off on makeing [sic] love when writing hard as the two things are run by the same motor." —
> Ernest Hemingway

"I write all my books slowly, with two fingers on an old typewriter, and the actual task of getting the words on paper is difficult. Nothing I write is good enough to be used in first draft, not even important personal letters, so I am required to rewrite everything at least twice. Important work, like a novel, must be written over and over again, up to six or seven times. For example, *Hawaii* went very slowly and needed constant revision. Since the final version contained about 500,000 words, and since I wrote it all many times, I had to type in my painstaking fashion about 3,000,000 words." —
James Michener

"I am a very slow writer. I have never done more than five or six good lines in a day." —W. B. Yeats

Some writers like to take their time. Writing about his multivolume American Chronicle series in a 1999 note to an edition of *Washington, D.C.*, Gore Vidal said that in 1962 he began to write about the Potomac in a summer storm in 1937.

"As I wrote, curious to know what was going to happen next, I had no idea that I had begun a work that has taken me, so far, thirty years *not* to finish."

With the seventh book in the series, *The Golden Age,* published in 2000, Vidal did get to finish.

Harper Lee moved to New York to write in 1949, working in an airline office to pay the bills. Some years later, a couple gave her enough money as a Christmas present to take a year off to write, money she later repaid. In a story in the *Chicago Tribune* for which Lee was photographed—she hasn't given an interview since the mid-sixties—it was noted that Lee still splits her time between Monroeville, Alabama, and Manhattan, which was where she had written *To Kill a Mockingbird,* her only book. Published in 1960, it sells about a million copies a year. In 1964 Lee was asked by Roy Newquist if she was working on another novel.

"Yes, and it goes slowly, ever so slowly . . . I like to write. Sometimes I'm afraid that I like it too much because when I get into work I don't want to leave it."

DEGREE OF DIFFICULTY

"Writing is hard, even for authors who do it all the time."
—Roger Angell

"PLAYBOY: What goes on in hell, Fran? What does it look like?
LEBOWITZ: Hell looks like the girls' gym at my high school. In
hell, I am taking gym, but I also have a book due."
—Fran Lebowitz

In his foreword to the fourth edition of *The Elements of Style*, Roger Angell writes how he would watch his stepfather, E. B. White, work hard to write his weekly "Notes and Comment" page for the *New Yorker*. No matter how many times he had fulfilled the assignment, it was never easy. E. B. White's famous advice in the last chapter of Strunk and White appears straightforward. "Be clear"—you can't get much simpler than that but, alas, none of it is easy.

"There is no such thing as a secure writer: every novel is an impossible mountain." —John le Carré

"My book is like going up a mountain. Each time I think I have reached the last rise another unfolds. . . . " —Owen Wister on writing *The Virginian*

"Even after writing *Mama, Disappearing Acts* and *Waiting To Exhale*, books don't get easier to write. It's not a formula." —Terry McMillan

"I rarely write easily. I could spend the whole day just trying to write a nice paragraph, and other days I write more but the work is no good. It's always a mysterious process." —Chang-rae Lee

They can be paraded, on and on, a seemingly unbroken procession of writers, some sounding more actively miserable than others.

"... for the most, writing is now just a horrible grim burden, I wouldn't do it if I were not morally engaged to do it." —Katherine Anne Porter

"Q: What do you like least about writing?
A: Most of all is the feeling of dread that I have. I always have another cup of coffee first." —Tobias Wolff

"I'm not convinced that many professional writers 'like' to write in the sense that they find writing to be fun—something that, in and of itself, yields pleasure. It may be absorbing, satisfying, even exhilarating, but it is hard work." —James B. Stewart

"My life has been in my poems. To make them I have broken my life in a mortar as it were." —W. B. Yeats

"But I don't know but a book in a man's brain is better off than a book bound in calf—at any rate it is safer from criticism. And taking a book off the brain, is akin to the ticklish and dangerous business of taking an old painting off a panel—you have to scrape off the whole brain in order to get at it with due safety—& even then, the painting may not be worth the trouble. —Herman Melville, *Letter to Evert Duyckinck*

These quotes are not designed to discourage—on the contrary. If the professional writer, even celebrated authors like those listed above, finds writing difficult, then it's okay for the rest of us too. There is perhaps a feeling that it *should* be hard work, that nothing that comes too easily is worth having. If a writer says he finds writing easy, then you can be justifiably envious ("good for you"), but also skeptical. Even the best struggle sometimes.

Realizing that writing well is difficult will also help you manage your expectations. If you start off exuberantly and allow thoughts of publication, riches, and a spot on the *Today Show* to take root, the inevitable lean periods will seem longer and the potholes deeper. Of course you should try to write, but don't think it's going to be easy and don't fantasize too much about the inevitability of your success.

Natalie Goldberg wrote *Writing Down the Bones,* one of the most popular of all popular writing books. Published in 1986, the book has sold more than a million copies. In 2001, she published *Thunder and Lightning,* whose first lines are cautionary:

"I have not seen writing lead to happiness in my friends' lives. I'm sorry to say this, I, who just fifteen years ago published a book telling everyone to grab their notebooks and write their asses off."

Of course, try, try, and try again. But no one ever said it was going to be easy.

All this notwithstanding, in *Escaping into the Open: The Art of Writing True*, Elizabeth Berg provides a fascinating list called "Myths to Ignore." Number One on the list is "Writing is hard," and it deserves to be mentioned. Berg says that some writers find writing hard; others not so.

"Don't let someone else's ideas about writing shape your own experience prematurely; don't let others' weary admonitions about the difficulty they've had in doing something in particular discourage you from trying yourself."

"It is hard but it's no harder than being a marvelous gymnast or a great singer or a marvelous anything else. If you have the ability and you perfect the discipline, the work can be done; it's simply a matter of sitting down and doing it. It's by no means unimaginably difficult; and I've had an extremely happy work life with very few days in which I haven't written, very few days in which the writing didn't produce more pleasure than pain. So I would absolutely argue against those people who say it was so difficult. I would just say those people are either under-talented or under-encouraged." —Reynolds Price

Writers can occasionally be found expressing satisfaction at what they have wrought:

"*The Last Precinct* is my favorite. It's the most powerful book I've written; it brings you right into Kay's soul and mind. This book is almost miraculous. I don't know how I did it, but I knew I wrote a good book." —Patricia Cornwell

"When I wrote the last line, I remember that I cried: 'Well, I'll never beat that,' and threw the inky pen at the opposite wall." Sir Arthur Conan Doyle on *The White Company*

And of one's first book, there is pride.

"No, indeed, I am never too busy to think of S&S [*Sense and Sensibility*]. I can no more forget, than a mother can forget her sucking child. . . . " —Jane Austen

PART 2

JOURNALISM

"Journalism: 'The daily opiate of the restless.'"
—Gay Talese, *The Kingdom and the Power*

"But there is a knack of writing for newspapers which has to be learned, and it is quite independent of literary merits."
—Virginia Woolf

Do you want your writing to make a difference? Do you want to ferret out stories and bring down the powerful and the corrupt? Do you want to be guaranteed hundreds of thousands of readers every time you publish? Do you want to be paid to write about what you think? Then be a journalist (or a columnist).

As Oscar Wilde famously wrote,

"The difference between literature and journalism is that journalism is unreadable, and literature is not read."

A lot of journalism *is* disposable—there's nothing as dead as yesterday's paper, but more practically-minded commentators, like William Zinsser, perhaps, might argue against both ends of Wilde's proposition from opposing viewpoints. Literature and journalism are apples and oranges; or, they are apples and apples. Regardless, each is *writing*, and journalism is one of the few fields involving writing that offers you a trade to go along with the vocation and the chance to make a living besides.

In *Newswriting and Reporting*, James M. Neal and Suzanne S. Brown write that "Every journalist, working in whatever medium of whatever level, is basically a reporter." Reporters learn tools that will be useful if you chose to write in a different form. Pete Hamill said as much about Robert Caro, who was once a reporter for *Newsday*:

> **"His time as a journalist has helped make him a better historian because he knows how to make the writing vivid, while simultaneously telling a story."**

The novelist Theodore Dreiser was a reporter for a short time. He wrote about visiting "one lithe, bony specimen of an editor" when he was looking for a job in Chicago:

> **"'Ever worked on a paper before?'**
> **'No, sir.'**
> **'How do you know you can write?'**
> **'I don't, but I think I could learn.'**
> **'Learn? Learn? We haven't any time to teach anybody here. You better try one of the little papers—a trade paper maybe, until you learn how—then come back,' and he walked off."**

When you find somewhere to train, you could, following Neal and Brown, use Rudyard Kipling's verse from "The Elephant's Child," one of the *Just So Stories*, as the key for sound practice:

> "I keep six honest serving men
> (They taught me all I knew)
> Their names are *what* and *why* and *when*
> And *how* and *where* and *who.*"

Kipling's honest men can serve you for any nonfiction, but only reporters are duty bound to keep in mind all six as they convey information to their readers. In Dickens's time, that could only be achieved using the printed word. Later, print journalists were joined by radio reporters. On radio, too, there's a package that includes voice and inflection, things that writers must convey in their writing. On television, the image comes first and second unless a commentator is talking straight at the camera. Then they're often said to be delivering an essay. Then we know it's a piece of writing that happens to be on TV.

When Charles Dickens was a reporter in the British Houses of Parliament, there were no recording devices. Part of Dickens's job was to copy important speeches so they could be reproduced in the newspaper—taking dictation, in other words. Many reporters will recognize the kinds of working conditions Dickens talked about when he reminisced at a dinner in 1865:

> "I have pursued the calling of a reporter under circumstances
> of which many of my brethren here can form no adequate

conception. I have often transcribed for the printer, from my shorthand notes, important public speeches in which the strictest accuracy was required, and a mistake in which would have been to a young man severely compromising, writing on the palm of my hand, by the light of a dark lantern, in a postchaise and four, galloping through a wild country, and through the dead of the night, at the then surprising rate of fifteen miles an hour. The very last time I was at Exeter, I strolled into the castle-yard there to identify, for the amusement of a friend, the spot on which I once 'took,' as we used to call it, an election speech of Lord John Russell at the Devon contest, in the midst of a lively fight maintained by all the vagabonds in that division of the county, and under such a pelting rain, that I remember two good-natured colleagues who chanced to be at leisure held a pocket-handkerchief over my note-book, after the manner of a state canopy in an ecclesiastical procession...." —John Forster, *The Life of Charles Dickens*

This sense of immediacy and excitement is what attracts many to reporting. The other side of that coin is described by Neal and Brown:

> "Reporters write about the here and now for readers in their own time. They have little prospect of wealth, and it is unlikely that anything they write will outlive them."

But, they add, "They have a front-row seat at the human comedy." It was the prospect of the front-row seat that got Theodore Dreiser hooked:

> "Because the newspapers were always dealing with signs and wonders—great functions, great commercial schemes,

great tragedies and pleasures—I began to conceive of them as wonderlands in which all concerned were prosperous and happy. Indeed, so brilliant did they seem—they and the newspaper world, as I thought of it—that I imagined if I could once get in it—if such a thing were possible—that I would be the happiest person imaginable. I painted reporters and newspapermen generally as receiving fabulous salaries, being sent on the most urgent, interesting and distingué missions. I think I confused, inextricably, reporters with ambassadors and prominent men generally. Their lives were laid among great people—the rich, the famous, the powerful—and because of their position and facility of expression and mental force they were received everywhere as equals, Think of me, new, young, poor, being received that way. How marvelous that would be." —Theodore Dreiser, *Newspaper Days*

Thanks to your writing, you can mix with these nabobs. If they behave badly and you catch them at it, you are first in line to embarrass them before the world. The first African-American reporter to spend a career at a major city paper was Ted Poston, who wrote for the *New York Post* from 1936 to 1972. He told his colleague Pete Hamill, "This is the best gahdamned business in the world. . . . We help more gahdamned people than any gahdamned government." And journalists can take down those in power too—ask Richard Nixon.

As for Theodore Dreiser, he was disillusioned by what he found in journalism when he got there.

"Journalism, like politics, as I was now soon to see, was a slough of muck, a heap in which men were raking busily and filthily for what they might uncover in the way of financial, social, political and publicity returns, such as those of fame or even passing applause."

If you have less lofty expectations than Dreiser's, you're less likely to be disappointed.

"I wanted to be a reporter because I enjoyed writing and reporting seemed like a good way to make a living, not as much fun as playing baseball but the best option available for someone with a weak arm who couldn't run." —Jack W. Germond, *Fat Man in a Middle Seat*

Jack Germond went on to be one of the best political reporters of his era.

Political reporting is a specialty, like criticism or obituaries or sports. In Richard Ford's novel *The Sportswriter*, Frank Bascombe writes a novel that's published to modest success, so he moves to New York to establish what he thinks of as a writing life for himself. He gets an advance for a second book and marries and starts a family. But along the way, Bascombe loses the thread and stops writing. In short, he's washed up. Then Bascombe gets a call from the managing editor of a magazine who offers him a job as a sportswriter. The editor assumed that Bascombe, as an American male, knew enough to do the job. More than anything, Bascombe reflects,

"... what you needed was a willingness to watch something very similar over and over again, then be able to write about it in two days' time, plus an appreciation of the fact that you're always writing about people who wanted to be doing

what they're doing or they wouldn't be doing it, which was the only urgency sportswriting could summon, but also the key to overcoming the irrelevancy of sports itself."

You can always turn to reviewing:

"They have offered me Clifton Fadiman's job reviewing books on *The New Yorker,* and I've decided to take it for a year, though I doubt whether anything good but money will come of it." —Edmund Wilson

Other specialists like columnists and editorial writers have earned the right to insert their opinions into their pieces. Erma Bombeck's enormously popular humor columns—she wrote more than 4,000—appeared in hundreds of newspapers around the country. Crafting a successful column is much harder than it looks, which is the case with all good writing. Bombeck told aspiring writers that she listed 'rewrite' as her occupation on her driver's license.

"It's supposed to sound like something that came off the top of my head as I was folding the laundry, and I thought, 'Oh God, I just want to say this.' That's not true at all."

In the final reckoning, it is the hope of being an eyewitness to something momentous that drives many reporters. In his book about the *New York Times*, Gay Talese writes about Tom Wicker, who was in Dallas on November 22, 1963, as part of the press corps following President Kennedy. When Kennedy was shot, the reporters were in a bus about ten cars behind the president's limousine. Wicker heard no shot but saw the pres-

At the 1992 Democratic national convention, Molly Ivins wrote a column in 24 minutes when Ross Perot dropped out of the race. What other piece of writing can be completed for publication satisfactorily in 24 minutes?

But if she didn't know exactly how to write a good column, Molly Ivins could never have pulled off the 24-minute trick. It is a particular kind of journalism.

The great newspaperman James Reston wrote columns, and after he retired, he received a large advance to write his memoirs. According to his biographer, Reston found it difficult to forget how to write like a columnist:

"The tone of the book was the same as the column had been. But the restraint and balance that made his columns so valuable made much of this memoir, in a time of self-revelation and personal vendetta, seem dated and pale."

ident's car take off fast. Wicker later said he *saw* the rumor of the event pass down through the crowd as people's heads turned to look for what they were hearing had happened.

Wicker's reporting took up more than a page in the next day's paper. For some reason, Wicker didn't have a notebook with him that day, and he had to scrawl notes on the back of an itinerary of the president's tour—notes that some days later he couldn't read. Wicker spent time in the hospital where

Kennedy was taken and sorted through the rumors and half-truths to write the story in the pressroom of the Dallas airport, where he ran with his typewriter and briefcase, jumping a fence on the way. Gay Talese said Wicker had reported better and written as well, but this was a test that could make or break a career.

> **"It is probably true that Wicker's reporting from Dallas that day, one afternoon's work, will live longer than any novel, or play, or essay, or piece of reportage that he has written or will ever write."**

Reporters will put themselves in perilous situations in search of a story, such as those war correspondents recently "embedded" by the hundreds with U.S. troops in Iraq. The Committee to Protect Journalists says that 366 journalists, including radio reporters, cameramen, and photographers, died in the ten years between 1993 and 2002.

One of the most famous journalists to be a casualty of war was Ernie Pyle, who was killed on the island of Ie Shima, near Okinawa, by Japanese machine-gun fire in April 1945. Pyle covered the war in Europe and the Pacific for the Scripps-Howard newspapers from 1940 and conveyed a real sense of what combat must be like by refusing to deny his own fear and anxiety. He was also a partial reporter.

> **"I have a sense that Pyle wrote for the men he walked beside, not for their superiors, not necessarily for their folks back home, certainly not for his publishers. He told his compatriots' stories honestly and forthrightly, and he consistently and unself-consciously used the personal pronouns I, we, my and**

ours in talking about their ventures." —Allan R. Andrews, *American Reporter*

One of Pyle's most famous pieces was about the death of Capt. Henry T. Waskow of Belton, Texas, who was killed in Italy in January 1944. Of all the officers Pyle had met, Captain Waskow was the most beloved by his men. Pyle's report conveys that plainly and with unabashed sentiment.

> **"Then the first man squatted down, and he reached down and took the dead hand, and he sat there for a full five minutes, holding the dead hand in his own and looking intently into the dead face, and he never uttered a sound all the time he sat there.**
>
> **"And finally he put the hand down, and then he reached up and gently straightened the points of the captain's shirt collar, and then he sort of rearranged the tattered edges of his uniform around the wound. And then he got up and walked away down the road in the moonlight, all alone."** —Ernie Pyle, "The Death of Captain Waskow"

According to Pyle's obituary in the *New York Times*, his writing was read in 14 million homes. According to the *Times*, he was so revered that "Soldiers' kin prayed for Ernie Pyle as they prayed for their own sons."

POETRY

"In the ninth grade a marvelous English teacher gave us
'Thirteen Ways of Looking at a Blackbird' by Wallace Stevens,
and she asked us to write a poem about the thirteen ways of
looking at something. I did an incredibly corny one. I wrote
about thirteen ways of looking at a rainbow. . . . And just the
idea of thirteen ways of looking at anything was thrilling to
me. So I began to write poetry. . . . "

—Deborah Garrison

Jorie Graham told Jim Lehrer how she became a poet: She
was hearing T. S. Eliot's "The Love Song of J. Alfred
Prufrock."

"I was studying film at New York University and lost my way
down a corridor one day, and I heard some words floating out
of the doorway . . . 'I have heard the mermaid singing each to
each, and I do not think that they will sing to me,' and I
thought, what is that? I just sank into the back seat of that
classroom and in some sense I think I've been sitting there
ever since."

Poets are often drawn to poetry by sound, the foundation of poetry.

"To make a poem, we must make sounds. Not random sounds, but chosen sounds." —Mary Oliver

"Well, I write with my voice. It's like improvising with jazz." —Robert Pinsky

"Poems start from a phrase, an image, an idea, a rhythm insistent in the back of the brain. I once wrote a poem when I realized I had been hearing a line from a David Byrne song entirely wrong, and I liked it my way." —Marge Piercy

"My introduction to poetry was through hip-hop. It was hip-hop first, [Nikki] Giovanni and [Amiri] Baraka second." —Saul Williams

"When I'm playing with words, I don't worry about sounding dumb or crazy. And I don't worry about whether or not I'm writing 'a poem.' *Word pool. World pool, wild pool, whip-poorwill, swing.* Words taken out of the laborious structures (like this sentence) where we normally place them take on a spinning life of their own." —Susan G. Wooldridge

As Mary Oliver describes in her book *A Poetry Hand-book*, the poet works with the notes of the alphabet that have their own sounds: "mutes, liquids, aspirates." There are devices you can employ as a poet that utilize the sounds: allit-eration, assonance, and so on. A poem is a particular form divided into lines and stanzas or running free.

Poetry operates on a different scale than prose. If the building block of prose is the sentence, in poetry it is a word or even a single sound.

"When I conduct poetry workshops, I ask the poets to take off all the modifiers and see what they have left. Often, what is left is more. The adjective can be a parasite that feeds off the noun and eventually kills it. There's nothing like a good noun standing there on its own. Cup. Hat. Bone. Each one tells its own long story. 'Chair' is an epic." —Billy Collins

"The only way one can ever really learn how to use any of these craft devices is to do endless exercises in notebooks: trying to master imagery, metaphor, simile, figure, conceit, assonance, alliteration, metrics, rhyme, diction, syntax, persona, and the various other techniques . . . " —William Packard

"A short poem is more difficult to write than a long one because a long poem acquires an impetus of its own. With each short poem one is making a fresh start and experiencing a new subject." —Wallace Stevens

Does it mean, if you are a poet, that you have a particular poetic sensibility?

"The true poetic temperament is that faculty that feels the most ordinary events of life as something wonderful and interesting, the most ordinary routine of life as something beautiful and significant." —Robert Hillyer

"Through its very being, poetry expresses messages beyond the words it is contained in; it speaks of our desire; it reminds

Working with the poetic form, you'll experience many of the concerns of any other writer, such as inspiration for your work and the flow of your writing.

"Prose, critical prose, examines and explains; its thrust is expository. Poetry dramatizes; its thrust is to present. But the secret of good prose is not that far from the secret of poetry, which is narrative." — Stanley Plumly

"The most important element of any poem is not its structure, rhyme, meter, line or language. It's the *idea*." — Michael J. Bugeja

"The process has very much unconscious work in it. The conscious process varies: my own experience is that the work as a poem 'surfaces' several times, with a new submergence after each rising." — Muriel Rukeyser

us of what we lack, of our need, and of our hungers. It keeps us dissatisfied. In that sense, it can be very, very subversive." —Adrienne Rich

"Poetry is the medium of choice for giving our most hidden self a voice—the voice behind the mask that all of us wear. Poetry says, 'You are not alone in the world: all your fears, anxieties, hopes, despairs are the common property of the race.'" —Stanley Kunitz

"I've often said that I don't think poetry is a particularly good form of expression. I know that goes against the grain, but I believe that. Photographs are more accurate. Theatre is more eloquent. But poetry is a superb, powerful and true form of experience. That's the satisfaction for me. I don't write a poem to express an experience. I write it to experience the experience." —Eavan Boland

"The poem, as it starts to form in the writer's mind, and on paper, can't abide any interruption. I don't mean that it *won't* but that it *can't.* . . . To interrupt the writer from the line of thought is to wake the dreamer from the dream." —Mary Oliver

"All the best things [a poet] ever uses are things he didn't know he was getting when he was getting them. A poet never takes notes. You never takes notes in a love affair." —Robert Frost to Cecil Day Lewis

Mary Oliver unites the concepts of *technique* that a good poet must master, and *sensibility* in a passage that stands for any writer. Oliver likens the creation of a poem to a romance such as that between Romeo and Juliet where one represents the head and the other the heart. No affair can proceed unless both lovers turn up for the assignation.

The part of the psyche that works in concert with consciousness and supplies a necessary part of the poem—the heat of a star as opposed to the shape of a star, let us say—exists in a mysterious, unmapped zone: not unconscious, not subconscious, but *cautious*. It learns quickly what sort of courtship it is going to be. Say you promise to be at your desk in the evenings, from seven to nine. It waits, it watches. If you are reliably there, it begins to show itself—soon it begins to arrive when you do. But if you are only there sometimes and are frequently late or inattentive, it will appear fleetingly or it will not appear at all.

Why should it? It can wait. It can stay silent a lifetime. Who knows anyway what it is, that wild, silky part of ourselves without which no poem can live? But we do know this: if it is going to enter into a passionate relationship and speak what is in its own portion of your mind, the other responsible and purposeful part of you had better be a Romeo. It doesn't matter if risk is somewhere close by—risk is always hovering somewhere. But it won't involve itself with anything less than a perfect seriousness.

For the would-be writer of poems, this is the first and most essential thing to understand. It comes before everything, even technique." —Mary Oliver

PLAYWRITING

"The theater is such a different game."
—Iris Murdoch, *Paris Review*

"How would she compare novel-writing with plays? 'I tell people it's the difference between corduroy and velvet: you can feel the difference, they come at you differently.'"
—Suzan-Lori Parks

The first stories were handed down by word of mouth and the first literature was oral.

"The very first people whom we consider authors—the minds and voices behind the tribal epics, the Bible and Homer, the Vedas and the sagas—were, it would seem, public performers, for whom publication took the form of recitation, of incantation...." —John Updike

Drama predates written fiction by thousands of years. The Egyptians staged dramas 4,000 years ago. Writing in the fourth century B.C., Aristotle described the difference between comedy and tragedy. So if you are interested in writing for the theater you are part of a 2,000-year tradition. The form has evolved, of course, but certain conventions have been established for a play: actors, direction, a stage, an audience. These are the elements Shakespeare had at his disposal. In Shakespeare you have perhaps the greatest of all writers, whose works are themselves a matchless muse:

> "No other writer has ever had anything like Shakespeare's resources of language, which are so florabundant in *Love's Labour's Lost* that we feel many of the limits of language have been reached once and for all. Shakespeare's greatest originality is in representation of character, however: Bottom is a wistful triumph; Shylock, a permanently equivocal trouble to all of us; but Sir John Falstaff is so original and so overwhelming that with him Shakespeare changes the entire meaning of what it is to have created a man made out of words." —Harold Bloom

> "We know there are rules for painting, music, dancing, flying, and bridge-building; we know there are rules for every manifestation of life and nature—why, then, should writing be the sole exception? Obviously, it is not." —Lajos Egri, *The Art of Dramatic Writing*

> "Central Character → Conflict/Dilemma → Resolution
> "This is the basic *structural* truth. When you strip away the elements that make each play unique—the use of language, theatricality, character personalities, humor, specifics of plot and setting—you're left with this basic *structure*.

That's why it's dramatic writing and not another form of fiction, like the novel or the short story." —Buzz McLaughlin, *The Playwright's Process*

In *How to Write a Play*, Raymond Hull quotes Goethe as saying that to learn the playwright's art, it is necessary to study Molière and he recommends Act II, Scene 9 of *The Imaginary Invalid*. "When one literary genius and man-of-the-theatre says of another, 'Look, here is the key to his success,' then ordinary writers should examine that key minutely." Hull says Molière has "all the elements of drama," which are six C's:

Conflict
Characters
Complications
Crisis
Catastrophe
Conclusion

The writer must take account of the role of the actor and all the issues involved in the staging of the production. The playwright's page is as flat and featureless as the novelist's, but when the drama takes to the stage, the dialogue and direction unfold on many levels. In *An Anatomy of Drama*, the critic Martin Esslin wrote that while a novelist has to describe what someone looks like, the playwright has an actor, the costume, and make-up do that. Literature has to operate on one level at a time, moving forward in a particular order while in drama several things can be happening. "Good morning my dear friend!" can, when spoken, be assigned hostility or sarcasm or

Lillian Hellman never saw a full performance of any of her plays once they opened. She'd drop by for half an hour once a week to make sure things were going okay.

> "The manuscript, the words on the page, was what you started with and what you have left. The production is of great importance, has given the play the only life it will know, but it is gone, in the end, and the pages are the only wall against which to throw the future or measure the past." — Lillian Hellman, *Pentimento*

any number of nuances. In a novel, the writer might have to say,

> "'Good morning my dear friend,' he said, but Jack had the impression that he did not really mean it. Was he sarcastic, he asked himself, or was he suppressing some deeply felt hostility..."

Playwrights might find the four-dimensional representation of their work to be liberating, or they might feel constrained by the need to rely on the interpretative powers of others—actors or a director—whose reading of their writing might not mirror their own.

> "The dramatist's principal interest being the movement of the story, he is willing to resign the more detailed aspects of the characterization to the actor and is often rewarded beyond expectation." —Thornton Wilder

"A famous novelist who asked to remain anonymous said after his one venture into playwriting that 'in the theater literature is never finished.'" —Frank Pike and Thomas G. Dunn

"A dramatist writes for the Theatre. A man who writes to be read and not to be performed is not a dramatist. The dramatist keeps in mind not the printer but a company of actors, not readers but playgoers." —J. B. Priestley

"It is not true to say that a play does not 'come alive' until it is actually in performance. Of course it comes alive—to the man who has written it, just as those three symphonies must have come alive to Mozart during those last six weeks." —John Osborne

"No leisure is permitted the audience to consider or digest what is happening on the stage. Comprehension must keep pace with what is occurring at every moment." —Bernard Grebanier

If you are writing for the theater, while wrestling with the specialties of the form you'll also be concerned with the tasks of creating characters in similar ways to the novelist.

"My writing is so character driven. I really take time to get to know the people who are in my plays; I understand their narrowness, their wideness. I have an intimacy with their cultural backgrounds and a feeling for how that affects their lives." —Wendy Wasserstein

"My characters make my play. I always start with them. They take spirit and body in my mind. Nothing they say or do is arbitrary or invented. They build the play about them like spiders weaving their webs." —Tennessee Williams

"Playwrights are either keen analytical psychologists—or they aren't good playwrights." —Eugene O'Neill

SCREENWRITING

> "An original screenplay? Nothing to it really.
> Just come up with a new and fresh and different story
> that builds logically on to a satisfying and surprising
> conclusion (because Art, as we all know, needs
> to be both surprising and inevitable).
> *Do you know how hard that is?*"
> —William Goldman

Novelists have long looked to Hollywood as a source of money. They've either worked on screenplays or polished up other people's work. Writers have also sold their stories to studios for development or adaptation. Most writers who are used to working alone complain about the process of screenwriting.

> **"Film writing, in the end, is committee work."** —Richard Russo

Screenwriting might make writers money, but it doesn't often make them happy.

Horton Foote was hired to write the screenplay for *To Kill a Mockingbird* and had a very happy experience working with the director, Robert Mulligan, the producer, Alan Pakula, and with Harper Lee. He was consulted about locations, sets, costumes, and casting.

> **"I thought, 'This is all very pleasant. Why are writers so unhappy out here?' Later, I learned the answer to that all too well."**

After a second, happy, job writing *Baby, the Rain Must Fall* for Mulligan and Pakula, things went downhill.

> **"There was a phrase, and I suppose still is, in the contracts of writers hired by studios that says in essence you are a writer for hire. They own what you have written and can edit and revise without your consent."**

William Faulkner's letters are full of complaints about Hollywood. He wrote to his agent about how depressed he felt there in 1931 while he was getting $10,000 to write a movie for Tallulah Bankhead. Faulkner did sign a seven-year contract with Warner Bros. but he wanted out of it.

> **"I have realised lately how much trash and junk writing for movies corrupted into my writing."**

Eventually, Faulkner worked with director Howard Hawks on *To Have and Have Not* and *The Big Sleep,* and when Faulkner's *Intruder in the Dust* sold to the movies for $50,000, he had the financial security he had long craved.

"I had to for the money." —John O'Hara

"We live in a culture in which writing the great American novel has been replaced by the desire to write the great American screenplay. Well, maybe not a *great* screenplay, but a script that generates a great deal." — D. B. Gilles

Of course, most screenwriters whose movies are made are professionals. The same is true of writers in television. Writing for movies and for television are two distinct entities that are cousins to the printed word as presented in book form. There are different disciplines and requirements to learn. Obviously, the visual element is the key difference.

"A screenplay is a story told in pictures." —Syd Field

"Writing for television, or teleplay writing as it is referred to in the industry, is an 'art of less,' the Zen of writing. Unlike the novel, the script is not 'complete.' It is a series of visual impressions giving the illusion of completeness." —Madeline DiMaggio, *How to Write for Television*

"The scene is, in a sense, a one-act play in itself, but one that dovetails with the preceding and subsequent scenes to form part of the larger screenplay." —David Howard and Edward Mabley, *The Tools of Screenwriting*

"A screenplay is like a noun—it's about a *person*, or persons, in a *place* or places, doing his or her or their '*thing*.' All screenplays execute this basic premise. The person is the character and his or her thing is the action." —Syd Field

Screenwriting has its own vigorous specialist literature and teaching program, like Robert McKee's Story Structure course, which says that alumni (perhaps 40,000 people have taken the course) have won 19 Academy Awards, 109 Emmy Awards, 19 Writers Guild of America Awards, and 16 Directors Guild of America Awards.

> **"What I teach is the truth: you're in over your head, this is not a hobby, this is an art form and a profession, and your chances of success are very, very slim."** — Robert McKee

> **"Reading screenplays is done by people who are looking for one to turn into a movie. These people *love* to make movies and *hate* to read. . . .**
>
> **"What these people read is a lot of bad screenplays, because 35,707 were registered last year with the Writer's Guild of America, about 99% of which are terrible."** —Denny Martin Flinn, *How Not to Write a Screenplay*

> **"The focus on conflict is so central to storytelling that it can be traced from the original Ten Commandments to the two film versions of the story."** —Ken Dancyger and Jeff Rush

Screenwriting, like writing for the theater, is ultimately a collaborative venture that involves actors, producers, directors, and craftspeople, none of whom has a direct equivalent in the literary world. Even the most persuasive book editor is not a director. In film, it is possible to write *for* someone (an actor), not just *about* them.

> "I wrote the part of Jules [in *Pulp Fiction*] for Samuel Jackson and of course Honey Bunny and Pumpkin for Amanda Plummer and [for] Tim Roth, who is one of my best friends."
> —Quentin Tarantino

> "My work in Hollywood has helped me very much. The good movie has to be written very clearly. The action has to be very clear. You can't take time out to digress to the highways and the byways of what might happen. You've got to tell the story. And I am trying to do this in my plays." —David Mamet

Although nothing would happen without him, the writer is somewhat less important than the director or the actor. Who are Julius J. Epstein, Philip G. Epstein, and Howard Koch? They are the three credited writers of *Casablanca*. There was a fourth writer, Casey Robinson, who juiced up the love interest but didn't receive a credit. The film is so much the property of Humphrey Bogart and Ingrid Bergman that the names of the writers and the director, Michael Curtiz, are scarcely recognizable to the general public.

> "I wrote eight scripts to get 'discovered.'" —Max Adams, *The Screenwriter's Survival Guide*

> "I wrote the book *Fast Times At Ridgemont High* and the studio told me, 'We're looking for the cheapest guy who can adapt your book. Do you feel like writing a screenplay?' I said,

'Sure. I'd pay you for the shot at that.' And essentially I did. I spent a lot of time for no money trying to teach myself how to write a script." —Cameron Crowe

"I insure my family's health through the Screenwriters Guild and you have to make a minimum amount every year as a screenwriter to keep your insurance up. I mostly do it for the insurance, actually. But this most recent one—I just got offered the chance to do *Spiderman II*, or to take a whack at it, I should say. I could have passed it up because I just finished the *Kavalier and Clay* screenplay, but I just couldn't resist." —Michael Chabon

WRITING COURSES

"A teaching community is ideal for a writer . . . we're constantly trading books, talking about things, and it's a lot like the way that a knife gets sharpened by constant friction against a stone."
—Tobias Wolff

"I'm doubtful about writing classes, but not entirely against them."
—Stephen King

Is it possible to learn how to write? One of the country's most prestigious writing schools is the University of Iowa Writers' Workshop, the first creative writing degree program in the country. The Workshop brochure states, "If one can 'learn' to play the violin or to paint, one can 'learn' to write, though no processes of externally induced training can ensure that one will do it well."

"Five thousand writing-class students who study 'required reading' can put their hand to the legend of Faustus but only one Marlowe was born to do it the way he did." —Jack Kerouac

Certainly the Iowa Writers' Workshop has attracted some impressive names to its faculty: Robert Penn Warren, Robert Lowell, John Berryman, John Cheever, James Alan MacPherson, Rita Dove, Jane Smiley, James Tate, Louise Glück, Philip Roth, Philip Levine, and Jorie Graham.

> **"The Writers' Workshop at Iowa is like any number of communities artists have gathered in for centuries—London, Paris, Barcelona, New York—to talk to each other, to formulate the goals of their hoped-for revolutions."** —Jorie Graham

On the faculty is Ethan Canin, author of *The Palace Thief* and *For Kings and Planets*, among other works. Canin studied at the workshop himself but suffered an inopportune and lengthy slump when he was there. He was able to produce only two stories in two years. "I panicked. I gave up. I realized I was never going to be a writer," he told *Stanford* magazine.

Canin went to Harvard Medical School and found he was able to write. His story collection *The Emperor of the Air* was published when he was a student, and he eventually gave up medicine to write, ending up back at Iowa, but on the faculty.

Another famous student was Flannery O'Connor. In an introduction to O'Connor's *Complete Stories*, Robert Giroux writes that O'Connor wrote six stories as part of the requirement for her M.F.A. degree and dedicated them to her teacher Paul Engle. When Engle first met O'Connor, he found her southern accent so impenetrable that O'Connor was forced to write, "My name is Flannery O'Connor. I am not a journalist. Can I come to the Writers' Workshop?"

Paul West has taught at Brown University, Cornell University, and the University of Arizona. West's book *Master Class: Scenes from a Fiction Workshop* is an impassioned, not to say combative book about learning and teaching. West is opinionated: "If there's a battle of the books, it was over long ago with the arrival of a huge skim-reading public that cares no more about sentences than about how an ostrich wipes its rear." Clearly, his class is not for the faint of heart:

> "I am tempted to tell them that the really hard work begins only after you finish writing, but I don't; they would never believe me anyway, convinced as most of them are that the golden caravanserai of print awaits them around the corner complete with keen editorial minds and benign contracts. What always bothers me is that, when you hone the average into being superior, you are making them less publishable; so what on earth do you do with as bright and gifted a bunch as this, already superior from reading and practice, ready to be, if lucky, virtuosos, some even with a distinctive style, that bright unique emanation from the personality? I have seen the enemy and they are not us. Thank Zeus, I say, for the handful of able editors, to whom the MBA remains a closed book, who still think publishing a noble vocation and revel in interior words. I suppress all this, if I can, believing as I must in the quality of prose as some doctors believe in quality of life. And I reserve the right, now and then, to tell some blockhead where to get off, I the 'legendary and ferocious' oracle who once told a writing student, now an editor at some magazine, 'I would rather lie naked in a plowed field, under an incontinent horse, than read this piece again.' Of such disdain is reputation made. Those who enter this room have guts." — Paul West, *Master Class*

John Gardner, author of *On Becoming a Novelist,* has written about the importance of a literary community to a writer.

> **"The writer who avoids writers' workshops (or some other solid community of writers) is in for trouble. One can be fooled by the legend of, say, Jack London, and imagine that the best way to become a writer is to be a seaman or lumberjack."**

London was "a relatively bad writer," Gardner has said. "He could have used a few teachers." Hemingway may have bolted to Paris, but he studied with Gertrude Stein; Joseph Conrad worked with Ford Madox Ford, H. G. Wells, Henry James, Stephen Crane, and so on. Some writers crave one another's company and congregate at places like Yaddo, the artist colony in Saratoga Springs, New York. Yaddo provides a close-typed nineteen-page list of all the writers who have spent time there since 1926.

> **"Writers are a bit like old buildings—we need a lot of shoring up."**—Val McDermid

Master Class includes a short introduction by Lisa Roney, who has published *Sweet Invisible Body: Reflections on a Life with Diabetes.*

> **"Within a matter of two months, I went from cranking out soured romantic stories to crafting a bizarre and tortured experimental piece about the experience of hypoglycemia, and all the credit goes to Paul, who pushed hard, whose spoken vocabulary wheeled like stars in the firmament, who gave me a photocopied page of Proust with the instruction to read it every night before I went to sleep."**

Anyone who will spend the money to attend a writing course must be serious about wanting to write. If you have the motivation, the program gives you the opportunity and a ready-made community of other writers to swap ideas with or compete against, depending on your inclination. So for that period, your job is to write and nothing else. Few nonprofessionals in the outside world have that opportunity.

> **"I cannot say often enough that the teaching of writing is Socratic. The end is not the production of clones of any approved style of writer—and certainly not of the teacher! The end is the full development of what is unique in the young writer, without encouraging him in mere eccentricity."** —Wallace Stegner

For the writing student, the crunch surely comes.

> **"Nearly every beginning writer sooner or later asks (or wishes he dare ask) his creative writing teacher, or someone**

else he thinks might know, whether or not he really has what it takes to be a writer. The honest answer is almost always, 'God only knows.'" —John Gardner

Occasionally, Gardner says, the answer is "yes," and now and then, it's "I don't think so."

"Teaching writing is a hustle." —Cormac McCarthy

"Please don't call this a course of 'creative' writing. I hate that word. Writing's writing and that's all there is to it." — Robert Frost on taking a teaching position at the University of Michigan

Lastly, the teaching of writing has an effect on the teacher as well as the pupil. Jayne Anne Phillips was talking about teaching a class when she said, "Teaching shoots writing in the head."

PUBLISHERS AND PUBLICATION

◎ ◎ ◎

"The profession of book-writing makes horse-racing seem like
a solid, stable business."

—John Steinbeck

"Mr. Murray's letter is come. He is a rogue of course,
but a civil one. He offers $450 [for *Emma*] but wants
to have the copyright of M.P. & S.& S. included.
It will end in my publishing for myself I daresay."

—Jane Austen

If publication is your goal, there will come, if all goes well,
a moment when all the hours and days and months of sleep-
deprived torment spent staring at blank pieces of paper will be
vindicated. You are ready to invite the world to read your
writing. And, you hope, buy it.

But first, hold on. Are you sure, are you really sure? You
are? Then put on your thickest skin and go for it.

Unless you pay someone, or do it yourself, there is no sure-
fire way to get a book, a story, or anything else published,
despite what some self-help manuals say. There are certainly
ways *not* to approach a magazine or a publisher, like using

scented pink paper or making threats. There are, alas, few positive pieces of advice that are actually helpful. The sorry fact is that it's often better to be lucky than to be good.

The first advice is that a literary agent can be instrumental, and the second is that a book publisher is much more likely to pay attention when you have already had something published in another medium. For fiction writers, the apogee of achievement is being published in the *New Yorker*. Fortunately, there is a vast array of other prestigious titles besides.

If you must, you can send your manuscript on spec to a major trade publisher in New York. Very rarely—almost never, in fact—is anything published from the "slush pile," which is where unsolicited manuscripts end up. Potential authors would be dispirited by the ziggurats of unread solicitations that inevitably form in the corridors of the few publishers that still accept them.

If you send your work anywhere—to an agent or a publisher, or to an agent to send to a publisher—*always* keep a copy. Also, you have to be prepared to wait and you shouldn't unduly elevate your expectations. Your proposal—an outline of your work, a sample, and a cover letter—must be neat and legible. Scour it for typos and mistakes with the spell-checker turned off, just as you would if preparing a resume. Avoid making barely sustainable claims about yourself or your work and don't bother mentioning bestsellers that your work resembles. (How many books can really be "like" *Seabiscuit*?) Stick to "This is who I am; this is my manuscript; I hope you like it."

"The best proposals are those that elicit the fewest questions. Why? Because you've anticipated and answered them

all. Remember, your aim is to write a proposal so gripping that after reading it an editor will get on the phone and offer you a contract for your book." —Jane von Mehren, *Editors on Editing*

"Your best bet, any way you look at it, is to force yourself to forget a script the moment it is put in the mail and concentrate on writing new material." —Scott Meredith (of the Scott Meredith Literary Agency)

"1. Don't take rejection personally. It's about their publishing needs, not about *you.*

2. Don't stop writing. If you love to write, keep writing. Rewrite the rejected piece or write something new. Just keep the pen on the paper." —Rachel Simon

Point number one is valid enough—the publisher may just have committed to three other first-time novelists and hasn't room for you. Buy you may well have poured so much of *you* into the writing that you can no longer distinguish between *you* and *your work* or you don't care to. Very well then, make hatred and revenge your muses and attack point number two with gusto.

"I started writing, and then I bought a book on where to send stories. I would send them out, they all came back, then I would write something else, this went on for years. Sometimes I got a nice note, and that gives you a little bit of inspiration for the next time you sit down to write. It's a combination of being attuned to that whole world out there, the editor, the publisher, blah, blah, blah, but also knowing that really is not the goal. If it happens, it happens; if it doesn't happen for a long time, that's okay too." —Jhumpa Lahiri

"What if after a number of submissions it turns out that nobody wants your work, does that mean it's no good? Not at all. Provided that someone of discernment has liked something about your work, it simply means that the milieu you thought you belonged to is inappropriate or not ready to accept you yet." —Nancy Bogen

Bogen, talking about magazines, goes on to say you should either look for different magazines or start your own.

If you are taken up by a publisher, chances are it will have come through the good offices of a literary agent. Literary agents will be able to help with the important task of acquainting yourself properly with the publishing business. Your editor is your point of contact with the rest of the company and is your advocate and your ally. It is their job, once they have convinced the publisher that they should acquire your work, to in turn convince everyone else in-house—marketers, salespeople, publicists, and so on—that your project is worthy and valuable.

The editor should also help you shape your book.

"I often tell people about the arrival of the edited manuscript of my first novel, *Mean Time*. I opened the envelope and there discovered the marginalia and emendations of my editor, who happened to be Toni Morrison. In glancing through

the pages, I felt like shouting: "My baby! My baby! What have you done to my baby!" —Christopher T. Leland

Once Leland looked at the changes and queries, he saw they were almost always an improvement.

Terry Brooks worked long and hard on a second book after the great success of *The Sword of Shannara*. He wrote 375 pages of a sequel called *The Song of Lorelei*, which Brooks sent to his editor, Lester del Rey, when he got a little bogged down. Brooks was flabbergasted when del Rey told him to abandon the book. But when del Rey returned the manuscript with closely argued comments inserted every three or four pages, Brooks concluded del Rey was right. He did drop *The Song of Lorelei*, salvaging one character and some settings for later use, and wrote *The Elfstones of Shannara*. Brooks said he learned more from that one experience than from all other writing experiences combined.

In *Publishers Weekly*, the editor Larry Ashmead described what happened when his colleague Tay Hohoff first read the manuscript of *To Kill a Mockingbird*:

> **"Hohoff read it and went to her boss and said, 'I want to take six months off and work on this book. I believe it could be one of the great novels of our age.' She got six months off, and Harper Lee gave her $5,000 for Christmas so she could do so. They worked each day. There was a lot of autobiography in that book, and a lot of editorial help. I think that's why Lee never wrote another book. It was a perfect collaboration; it shows publishing at its very best."**

Copyeditors and the production staff (a category that may include copy, design, and art departments) get the book after the editor. The copyeditor will probably make it more grammatically consistent and stylistically a piece. Designers and artists work to create an attractive package—something that will stand out in a bookstore and say, "Buy me."

"The author or translator is supposed to turn in the manuscript in a form ready for the printer. But no author, in the history of printing, has been able to do that ..." —Datus C. Smith, Jr., *A Guide to Book Publishing*

Once your book is in production and you are in the downtime before publication, you might be asked to perform certain authorial tasks, such as preparing author questionnaires and reading-group guides. Later, if your sales merit, you may take part in publicity at events like conventions, interviews, and signings. Each of these functions is designed to sell books, which is only to your advantage, although a surprising number of authors place severe limitations on the amount of promotion they are willing to do. Publishers' resources are limited, and if you don't play ball, there'll always be a cooperative author who will.

Again, you can be more helpful if you find out a little about the business. Some authors berate their publishers when they don't see copies of their book in the stores or when it doesn't get reviewed in the *New York Times*. Publishers cannot force bookstores to order your books; nor can they ensure that a book gets a review, much less a good one.

In the author/publisher relationship, there are a couple of rules. One is that if a small number of books are printed upside-down or have parts of another book inserted halfway through, these are the ones that the author will receive, and there will never be uncorrected copies of his book in the local store.

> "It is a commonplace joke—it is not a joke at all, they mean it bitterly—among editors and publishers that it would be a nice business if it were not for authors. That goes double the other way about, I think; and I am not joking either. . . . " —
> *Katherine Anne Porter*

> "One might say that the effective editor is on comfortable terms with God and with Mammon." —Gerald Howard, *Editors on Editing*

God in this case was represented on earth in the form of Maxwell Perkins, the famous Scribner's editor. Perkins's biographer A. Scott Berg conferred upon him the "G" word—genius—in the title of his book, *Max Perkins: Editor of Genius.* Perkins signed up, edited, befriended, was confessor to, bailed out, and generally looked after three of America's greatest writers: Fitzgerald, Hemingway, and Thomas Wolfe.

In 1918 Perkins persuaded his reluctant employers to publish Fitzgerald's first novel, *This Side of Paradise.* He worked closely with Fitzgerald on his other books, including *The Great Gatsby,* which Fitzgerald wanted to call *Trimalchio at West Egg.* Perkins was always respectful and had marvelous creative instincts, which he conveyed with simplicity. On Gatsby:

> "Couldn't *he* be physically described as distinctly as the others, and couldn't you add one or two characteristics like the use of that phrase 'old sport,' not verbal, but physical ones perhaps."

A s in any business, the relationship between an author and publisher can be strained by money. In *At Random*, Bennett Cerf describes what happened when his colleague Horace Liveright sold Theodore Dreiser's *An American Tragedy* to Hollywood for $85,000. Liveright and Dreiser had shaken hands on a deal whereby Liveright would get half of any money above $50,000. Dreiser always thought his publishers were ripping him off, so when Liveright told him of the deal over lunch at the Ritz, Dreiser was apoplectic that Liveright was getting $17,500 of his money and threw a cup of hot coffee over his publisher. Liveright turned to Cerf, who was present. "Bennett," Liveright said, "let this be a lesson to you. Every author is a son of a bitch."

Fitzgerald recommended Hemingway to Perkins (or "Hemmingway," as Fitzgerald spelled his name for a while) and they worked together. Perkins also wrestled Thomas Wolfe's books *Look Homeward, Angel* (1929) and *Of Time and the River* (1935) into publishable form. *Look Homeward, Angel* began life as *O Lost* and was a manuscript of 1,114 pages and 330,000 words, almost every one of which Perkins and Wolfe fought over, to the extent that Wolfe came to resent his reliance on his editor's talents.

Perkins was intimately involved in his writers' lives. One day in 1928, Hemingway's mother, Grace, asked Perkins to help locate her son to tell him his father had died. Within an hour, Perkins happened to get a telegram from Hemingway, who had stopped off on his way to Florida to ask his editor to wire him $100.

It is pointless to lament the fact that there aren't editors like Perkins "any more," because he was unique, just as Fitzgerald and Hemingway were each unique. Writer/icons like these do not exist in the same way in the modern culture.

Even if they are not Maxwell Perkins, editors at publishing houses are smart men and women who know about writing and about their business. Alas, editors have many more responsibilities beyond reading manuscripts and finding new writers. When they might be reading your novel, they are probably in a marketing meeting or rewriting jacket copy.

Writers might also wish to acquaint themselves with trends in the business of book publishing that have a direct effect on the number of titles that are published and how intellectual property is evaluated. Publishing companies that have been brought into large conglomerates must try to be more businesslike in a trade that resists outright commercialization. As Jason Epstein, former editorial director of Random House, writes,

> "Conglomerate budgets require efficiencies and create structures that are incompatible with the notorious vagaries of literary production, work whose outcome can only be intuited. How, for instance, does a corporation budget for Norman Mailer's next novel or determine the cash value of such writers as William Faulkner or Cormac McCarthy, whose novels languished for years before they became valuable assets on the Random House backlist?"

> "Why, there are Johnny-come-latelies in publishing now, as there were not in the sixties, who talk blithely of a 25 percent profit, whereas the house of Gallimard in Paris counts itself lucky to squeeze out 3. Above all, runs this slimy message: Do not challenge the reader with a long sentence, an unusual word, a passage of interiority. Writing for such people is to eat the recipe, not the meal." —Paul West

Publishing will never be a science. Publishers make mistakes about writers all the time, understandably because the book-buying public is extremely unpredictable and fickle. This might be of comfort to someone rejected by a publisher who has railed against the publisher's stupidity.

> "William Kennedy, . . . whose novel *Ironweed* won two of its year's three main prizes for fiction, has confided in accepting one of them that this novel was rejected by publishers thirteen times. The annals of modernism abound in such horror stories: no less a first reader than André Gide turned down, for Éditions Gallimard, *Swann's Way*, the first volume of Proust's sublime *Remembrance of Things Past*, whose publication Proust then undertook to finance himself; and not only did James Joyce's *Ulysses* have to be privately printed in France, but his exemplary book of short stories, *Dubliners*, now standard fare for high-school students, went unpublished for ten years while English and Irish printers dithered over a few of its excessively accurate details." —John Updike, *Odd Jobs*

Gilbert Sorrentino, author of the novels *Blue Pastoral* and *Little Casino*, has received critical plaudits and prestigious Lannan and Guggenheim awards. His books are difficult and experimental, and his novel *Mulligan Stew* was turned down by 28 publishers until Grove Press picked it up in 1979. Sorrentino told *Publishers Weekly* about one letter his agent Mel Berger received:

> "'Dear Mel: Thanks so much for allowing me to read Gil Sorrentino's new novel. It may well be the finest novel ever to cross my desk in 20 years of editing. Of course, we can't publish it.' That kind of thing has happened with many of my books."

In her autobiography, New Zealander Janet Frame wrote about visiting England in the 1950s. She met a group of young literary types who were astonished to hear that Frame had actually had two books published in New Zealand—a book of short stories and a novel. They asked the name of the publisher.

> "Their excitement about meeting a published author lessened as they admitted they had chosen their one and only publisher: Faber and Faber. Nothing less than Faber and Faber."

If you have your heart set on one publisher and it falls through, you can self-publish. There are many sources of helpful advice that will help you navigate the many new disciplines you'll have to tackle. Not only do you have to write the manuscript and create the finished book and manufacture copies of it, but you also have to distribute and market the book. Selling copies out of the trunk of your car is a tough way to recoup your investment.

"The feeling is exhilarating, the rewards are great, and the process is a lot simpler than it may seem. Not necessarily easy, mind you, but simple." —Tom and Marilyn Ross (Founders of the Small Publishers Association of North America)

In *How to Publish, Promote, and Sell Your Own Book*, Robert Lawrence Holt notes an impressive array of author-published books, among them Strunk's original *Elements of Style,* Twain's *Huckleberry Finn,* Edgar Rice Burroughs's Tarzan books, and Whitman's *Leaves of Grass.*

More recently, James Redfield's *The Celestine Prophecy* began as a self-published book, as did Richard Paul Evans's *The Christmas Box* and *Term Limits,* the first effort of thriller writer Vince Flynn.

AGENTS

"Don't have a literary agent.... Agents seem
somehow to be not quite human."
—Katherine Anne Porter

"My opinion of agents is frankly low."
—John O'Hara

John O'Hara's complaints about agents were many. In a letter to his friend Walter S. Farhquar, O'Hara wrote about
what he thought was habitual sharp practice. Neither did
he think an agent had ever sold anything that wouldn't
have been bought on its own merits. And while an agent
might say a publisher was excited by a story and would get
back to them any day, he'd believe it when he endorsed
the check. Boiled down, his advice amounted to "Don't sign
anything."

Eugene O'Neill was more sanguine. Giving advice to his
son, he wrote:

> "A good reliable agent costs you ten per cent but the money may be worth all he gets and more in terms of helping you help yourself *commercially* and you can always veto anything he digs up that you don't like."

A top-line literary agent will help you get in the door at the major publishers. Anything from William Morris or International Creative Management or a fairly long list of reputable agents and agencies gets read and considered. An agent's job is not just to sell your work to publishers but to support you as you write and to help you establish a career. For their 10 or 15 percent, they'll deal with royalty statements and 1099 forms; they'll call a publisher to ask what the marketing plans are for your book and even, at a lofty level, and to publishers' eternal irritation, what advertising they are taking out in the *New York Times*. (Publishers don't think ads in newspapers sell books.) Experienced agents should be thinking a book or two ahead of their clients.

Needless to say, unless you are a celebrity or someone in the news, you must have some decent writing to show the agent to get him or her interested in you in the first place. If fame is somehow thrust upon you suddenly, don't worry—the agents will be calling you.

There are a number of resources like the *Literary Marketplace* (*LMP*) that list agents and describe their specialties. J. K. Rowling picked some agents out of the British equivalent of the *LMP* in her local library in Edinburgh and included Christopher Little because she liked his name. Rowling sent Little and others *Harry Potter and the Philosopher's Stone*. Little wrote back and took it on. The agency's office manager told the *Daily Telegraph* she was permitted to make only a couple of photocopies of the manuscript to save money. Little eventually sold the book to U.K. publisher Bloomsbury for the equivalent of about $4,000. The *Daily Telegraph* reckoned Christopher Little's agency had made at least £15 million (approximately $24 million) from the series even before the fifth Potter book was published.

Occasionally the publishing stars align just right. When Alice McDermott had just started a novel, a friend who had encouraged her to write knew the agent Harriet Wasserman (a useful friend) and contacted her on McDermott's behalf.

> **"So I hand-delivered the manuscript because I felt so foolish even bringing it to the post office; I literally slipped it under Harriet's door and ran away. Then Harriet called and asked if we could meet, and suggested sending the book to Jonathan Galassi, who had just been made a senior editor at Houghton Mifflin. I had 100 pages, literally only 100 pages, not even page 101, by the time I went down to Jonathan's office. And I had a contract in another week."** —Alice McDermott, *The Book That Changed My Life*

Betsy Lerner points out that McDermott's first novel, *The Bigamist's Daughter,* was lauded on publication on the front page of the *New York Times Book Review* by Anne Tyler.

Laura Hillenbrand, who had written for *Equus* magazine for some years, wrote an award-winning article about Seabiscuit for *American Heritage* magazine. Quickly, she had a book deal and a movie deal, both before she'd written a line of the book.

"It was initially frightening. People think I must have been turning cartwheels on the night I sealed the movie deal—which was only two days after sealing the book deal—but I was really quite terrified. I spent a while circling around the lawn of the house where I was dogsitting, settling my stomach. My teeth were chattering."

GETTING PAID

"No man but a blockhead ever wrote except for money."
—Samuel Johnson

"You will be glad to hear that every Copy of S. & S. is sold & that it has bought to me £140 besides the Copyright, if that sh'd ever be of any value. —I have now written myself into £250—which only makes me long for more."
—Jane Austen

Samuel Johnson makes a blockhead of nearly everyone in publishing. Almost no one makes a lot of money from the business of books. In many ways, publishing is hardly a business at all. Its profit margins have traditionally been paper-thin, despite the best efforts of numerous conglomerates, near-exploitative salaries, and odd business practices. (In publishing, most of the product is determined by supply—the editors—rather than demand—the marketers.)

As for writers, a tiny few who receive an inordinate share of the limelight and most of the shelf space are compensated lavishly. But most authors, even those whose book is picked

The way it works is that a publisher pays a book advance, which is a payment made against future sales. The author earns a royalty on each sale, usually 15 percent for a hardcover book, less for a paperback. The royalties accrue until they have "broken even" or "earned out" the advance. An advance of $90,000 will earn out on net sales of 30,000 books where the cover price is $20.00 and the royalty is 15 percent. Publishers hold back money in anticipation of "returns," which are unsold books sent back from the bookstores for credit.

up by a major publisher, have no guarantee of making anything approaching stay-at-home money.

In 1990 Jeffrey Archer signed a five-book deal that paid him an advance of just £1 for each of his next five novels, meaning he'd "earn out" on the first book he sold. The $12 million President Bill Clinton reportedly received for his memoir will be more difficult to recoup.

When calculating an advance, publishers figure out how many copies they think they can sell. A very good net sale for a first novel might be 5,000 copies, which might translate to an advance of $15,000 before paperback money is considered.

Stephen King, on the other hand, receives something like $25 million per book these days, some 10,000 times more than he received for *Carrie*, his first novel, in 1974. In his memoir *On Writing*, he recalls his first decent paycheck:

"One day late in my final semester at college, finals over and at loose ends, I recalled the dyehouse guy's story about the rats under the mill—big as cats, goddamn, some as big as *dogs*—and started writing a story called "Graveyard Shift." I was only passing the time on a late spring afternoon, but two months later *Cavalier* magazine bought the story for two hundred dollars. I had sold two other stories previous to this, but they had brought in a total of just sixty-five dollars. This was three times that, and at a single stroke. It took my breath away, it did. I was rich."

Also in King's rarefied air is J. K. Rowling, whom the British press described in 2003 as being worth £310 million ($490 million). She earned £30 million ($47 million) of that when the fifth Harry Potter book was published around the world. These numbers correspond to those of other entertainment superstars. For example, the Associated Press reported that the actress Cameron Diaz made $42.2 million in 2001.

More representative of the usual writing experience is someone who toils for little reward or none. Obviously, if a writer cannot sell his work, he's forced to make his living somewhere else. Even when they do get paid, the rewards can be meager in comparison to the time and mental energy expended. In his twenties, George Bernard Shaw wrote four novels that were rejected by publishers. He earned £6 ($9.50) for a million words. Shaw did better later. William Faulkner, John O'Hara, and Wallace Stevens found cause to comment on their finances:

"I have 60¢ in my pocket and that is literally all." —William Faulkner

"I have exactly $5.55 in the world. . . ." —John O'Hara

"My royalties for the first half of 1924 amounted to $6.70. I shall have to charter a boat and take my friends around the world." —Wallace Stevens

A job that can be described as a "vocation" is often an ill-paid one in which the limited prospects of remuneration are not that important. If you agree with the following statement, you might see writing as a vocation.

"The defining characteristic of the literary vocation may be that those who possess it experience the exercise of their craft as its own best reward, much superior to anything they might gain from the fruits of their labors." —Mario Vargas Llosa

"Is literature really a profession?" —Wallace Stevens

A few writers have the wherewithal to adjust their writing to suit the market. Mario Puzo spent nine years writing *The Fortunate Pilgrim*, which was published to strong reviews but limited sales. Puzo said he "looked around and [I] said . . . I'd better make some money," and wrote the more commercial *The Godfather*, which Putnam bought for $5,000 in 1967. When the publisher sold paperback rights for $410,000, Puzo's gambit paid off.

It might be of some consolation to know that this has always been the case. In 1873 English philosopher John Stuart Mill wrote:

"Those who have to support themselves by their pen must depend on literary drudgery, or at best on writings addressed to the multitude; and can employ in the pursuits of their own choice, only such time as they can spare from those of necessity; which is generally less than the leisure allowed by office occupations, while the effect on the mind is far more enervating and fatiguing." —John Stuart Mill, *Autobiography*

So if you need money, try something else first.

Occupational Hazards

"Of the seven native-born Americans awarded the Nobel Prize in literature, five were alcoholic." (Sinclair Lewis, Eugene O'Neill, William Faulkner, Ernest Hemingway, John Steinbeck)
—Tom Dardis

"Writer's block is going to happen to you. You will read what little you've written lately and see with absolute clarity that it is total dog shit."
—Anne Lamott

For a sedentary and often solitary activity, writing has a surprising number of occupational hazards. Some can be injurious to the writer's health, not to mention his peace of mind.

Mind Alteration

In *The Thirsty Muse*, Tom Dardis speculated that the writing careers of Fitzgerald, Hemingway, and Faulkner were all curtailed by a reliance on alcohol. Writers have used alcohol and other drugs as a means of support and a means of inspiration. Ken Kesey experimented with peyote and other drugs when he was working nights at the Menlo Park Veterans Hospital, experiences that he wrote into *One Flew over the Cuckoo's Nest*. About Kesey, Tom Wolfe wrote, "Sometimes he would go to work high on acid. He could *see into their faces*."

> **"Writers have always used drugs and drink to disinhibit themselves. In the beginning, the intoxicating effects of alcohol and drugs can prove prodigious. But once the tail is wagging the dog, the effects are generally deleterious."** —Betsy Lerner

> **"Writer's block is a fancy term made up by whiners so they can have an excuse to drink alcohol."** —Steve Martin, *Writing Is Easy*

Writer's Block

The creative process is unpredictable. What can flow with marvelous ease one day can become inexplicably frozen solid the next. You have to hope that the new day will bring relief, but dry spells can run to droughts that can take a damaging toll on a writer's fragile self-confidence. While it might be tempting to seek solace in the bottle, the literature of writing is replete with suggestions for getting the flow back.

> **"Find a Cave; Phone a Friend; Put up with Imperfection..."** —*Stephen Frank, The Pen Commandments: A Guide for the Beginning Writer*

> **"Today, I will write even if all I do is jot down some notes about my feelings. I am storing up material for the future,**

without knowing what it is." —Susan Shaughnessy, *Walking on Alligators*

"**I think when you hit a place where you can't write you probably should be still for a while because it's not there yet.**"
—Toni Morrison

Losing Your Work

Many writers who work on a computer habitually back up copies of their work on disk. There is no excuse not to. It's worth saying again: You mustn't send your only original copy anywhere, under any circumstances. Even if you have written on a legal pad with a quill pen, you must photocopy your work before you part with it, whatever the expense. The consequences of loss have always been disastrous. In the era of carbon paper and typewriters, keeping a copy was more difficult but just as necessary.

In 1922 Ernest Hemingway's wife, Hadley, traveled from Paris to Lausanne, in Switzerland, where her husband was skiing. Hadley decided to bring all of Hemingway's unpublished work with her and packed everything—every manuscript and every copy—in a suitcase that was then stolen from her train at the Gare de Lyon in Paris. When Hadley got to Switzerland, she couldn't tell Hemingway right away what had happened. When he did find out, Hemingway returned at once to Paris to see if anything could be saved, but there was nothing, no trace of eleven stories, a novel, and some poems.

Hemingway wrote about the incident in *A Moveable Feast* more than thirty years later and downplays it, but Hemingway's biographer Jeffrey Meyers, who provided the basis of this account, said Hemingway was devastated and thought he might never write again. Meyers says Hemingway never forgave Hadley.

When T. E. Lawrence lost the manuscript of *The Seven Pillars of Wisdom* at the rail station at Reading in England, it was said that he sat down and didn't rest until he had rewritten the whole thing from memory.

Katherine Anne Porter lost the first two pages of a story she'd started and tried to re-create the two pages as she remembered. The story itself remained unwritten. Years later, Porter was rearranging some papers and the long-lost pages miraculously reappeared. Porter compared the original with the pages she had rewritten and found she'd made an almost perfect reproduction.

It's traumatic enough to lose two pages, but 2,604? In this case, fortunately, the victim is fictional. In Michael Chabon's *Wonder Boys*, Grady Tripp, a writing teacher, is struggling to finish a novel of the same name, seven years in the writing and "two thousand six hundred and eleven pages, each of them revised and rewritten a half dozen times." Grady Tripp's editor, Terry Crabtree, visits Tripp's university for a writing festival. Part of the novel's climax sees Crabtree driving madly in circles with the liberated pages of the manuscript of *Wonder Boys* flying into the air. Tripp saves six and a half pages:

> "'Naturally you have copies,' said Crabtree.
> I didn't say anything.
> 'Tripp?'
> 'I have earlier drafts,' I said. 'I have alternate versions.'
> 'You'll be alright then,' he said.
> 'Sure, I will. It'll probably come out better next time.'

'That's what they all say,' he said. 'Look at Carlyle, when he lost his luggage.'

'That was Macaulay.'

'Or Hemingway, when Hadley lost all those stories.'

'He was never able to reproduce them.'

'Bad example,' said Crabtree."

Falling out of Fashion

Literary taste is always inexplicable. To the roster of under-appreciated writers who could barely get published in their lifetime, if at all, we must add the victims of literary taste who are published and then become overlooked. William Faulkner, now an American staple, complained in 1945 that everything he had written other than *Sanctuary* was out of print. If you are published, hope to reach canonical status in time to enjoy the rewards that come with the approbation.

Consider these two lists of books:

One:

Guard of Honor by James Gould Cozzens

The Way West by A. B. Sloane

The Town by Conrad Richter

Andersonville by MacKinlay Kantor

The Travels of Jaimie McPheeters by Robert Lewis Taylor

Advise and Consent by Allen Drury

The Edge of Sadness by Edwin O'Connor

Two:

The Caine Mutiny by Herman Wouk

The Old Man and the Sea by Ernest Hemingway

A Fable by William Faulkner

A Death in the Family by James Agee
To Kill a Mockingbird by Harper Lee

The connection is that these lists comprise the winners of the Pulitzer Prize for fiction between 1949 (*Guard of Honor*) and 1962 (*The Edge of Sadness*). (There was no award in 1954 or 1957.) The difference is that some of the books in the first list are no longer in print, and the others only barely, their writers having gone out of fashion. The books in the second list enjoy robust health and sales.

Where lies the hazard to you? A writer's popularity might not coincide with his or her lifespan. If you think you are ahead of your time, you may be right. Sadly, you may not be around long enough to see vindication.

Plagiarism

> "The plagiarist is, in a minor way, the cop who frames innocents, the doctor who kills his patients. The plagiarist violates the essential rule of his trade. He steals the lifeblood of a colleague." —David Plotz, *Slate*

David Plotz was writing about historian Stephen Ambrose, passages of some of whose books were found to closely resemble passages of other books by other people that had already been published. As we have seen, fiction writers have influences. And nonfiction writers depend on sources, many of which are other books, which have themselves used published accounts in their own creation. The writer should avoid plagiarism. In turn, a hazard of writing is that anything one writes is subject to plagiarism.

Plagiarism can be difficult to define:

> "As with pornography, people think they know plagiarism when they see it. However, the definition of plagiarism changes depending on the writer's role and motivation. In his own self-defense, Oscar Wilde once stated, 'What the critic calls an echo is really an achievement.'" —Thomas Mallon, *Stolen Words: The Classic Book on Plagiarism*

Excellent sources for specific help in avoiding plagiarism are university Web sites. Colleges are eager to help their students prepare papers with the sources properly identified and attributed. Northwestern University defines *plagiarism* as "submitting material that in part or whole is not entirely one's own work without attributing those same portions to their correct source." And Drew University offers examples, quoting the following passage,

> "Such 'story myths' are not told for their entertainment value. They provide answers to questions people ask about life, about society and about the world in which they live." — *from* Davidson, Robert. *Genesis 1-11*. Cambridge: Cambridge UP

A paraphrase would be,

> "Specifically, story myths are not for entertainment purposes; rather they serve as answers to questions people ask about life, about society and about the world in which they live."

But,

> "This is an example of plagiarism as defined by the Drew University Academic Integrity Policy. The student copied words

Mallon was quoted in a story on plagiarism in *Poets and Writers* magazine in 2002: "A Brief History of the 'P' Word" by Julia Kamysz Lane. Mallon said one of the worst examples he knew was poet Samuel Taylor Coleridge, who plagiarized the German philosophers Immanuel Kant, Moses Mendelssohn, Friedrich von Schelling, Friedrich von Schlegel, and others. "I don't know [what's worse]," Mallon said, "Coleridge's plagiarism or the degree to which scholars tied themselves up in knots explaining it away," he says.

and phrases from the original without acknowledging their source."

Literary Spats

The literary spat is a perennial sport and pastime for writers. A three-on-one spat developed in recent years between Tom Wolfe on the one hand and John Irving, Norman Mailer, and John Updike on the other. Highlights included Wolfe labeling the others "The Three Stooges" and Mailer and Updike "two piles of bones." Updike and Mailer had both given negative reviews to Wolfe's *A Man in Full*. In the *New York Review of Books*, Mailer wrote,

"At certain points, reading the work can even be said to resemble the act of making love to a three-hundred-pound woman. Once she gets on top, it's over. Fall in love, or be asphyxiated."

"To be a writer in America is a contact sport. You've got to be tough." —Pat Conroy

Bad Reviews

The bad review is a constant occupational hazard. While Norman Mailer, as we have seen, has not been averse to giving a bad review, he has also written,

> "*Meretricious, dishonest, labored, loathsome, pedestrian, hopeless, disgusting, disappointing, raunchy, ill-wrought, boring*—these are not uncommon words for a bad review. You would be hard put to find another professional field where criticism is equally savage. Accountants, lawyers, engineers, and doctors do not often speak publicly in this manner."

Rosemary Mahoney spoke to *Publishers Weekly* about her experience with critics. Mahoney's *A Likely Story* was criticized for being unkind to its unkind subject, Lillian Hellman. Then Mahoney's *Whoredom in Kimmage* was thought to be too revealing of its Irish subjects.

"At this point I have stopped reading reviews, which isn't easy to do. In the end, you cannot control what people think about you. You have to be who you are."

"It is a terrible power that a writer imagines critics have, but it's just imagination. Any review (even unfavorable) is useful

because it mentioned the book and helps bring it to the reader's consciousness." —Isaac Asimov

In the summer of 2003, the British novelist Tibor Fischer wrote a newspaper article decrying Martin Amis's then-unpublished novel *Yellow Dog*. Fischer said the book was terrible and described it as "not-knowing-where-to-look bad"—and "It's like your favourite uncle being caught in a school playground, masturbating."

Managing Your Own Legacy

It is rare that a writer's reputation is enhanced by anything published long after he has died, especially any "newly discovered" text. If your massive novel was never published in your lifetime, and you didn't want it to be seen, you might want to get rid of it. In rare cases, writers' destruction of their own work has been a literary tragedy, as when Nikolai Gogol burned the final version of the second part of *Dead Souls*.

In the years since Ernest Hemingway killed himself in 1961, five full-length books by Hemingway have been published: *A Moveable Feast* (1964), *Islands in the Stream* (1970), *The Dangerous Summer* (1985), *The Garden of Eden* (1986), and *True at First Light*, published in 1999 to coincide with the centenary of the author's birth.

Where a legendary writer is concerned, the urge to publish as much as possible is understandable, although everything so produced should bear an asterisk in the reference books (* *started but never completed by author*).

Albert Camus died in a car accident in 1960. In a briefcase nearby was found the incomplete manuscript of a novel called

The First Man. The fragment was published in France in 1994 by Camus's daughter Catherine, who explained,

> "We believed a manuscript of such importance would sooner or later be published unless we destroyed it. Since we had no right to destroy it, we preferred to publish it ourselves so that it would appear exactly as it was."

Censorship

Of a different order from self-inflicted occupational hazards are the external perils a writer can face as a result of what he or she has written. These dangers fall under the general heading of censorship, although that is a beast that takes many forms.

Many, many writers remain unpublished or underpublished because of censorship. It is impossible to know how many writers preempt the censor and never put pen to paper in the first place.

Mikhail Bulgakov ran afoul of censors in Stalin's Soviet Union. He had worked on his novel *The Master and Margarita* for years, revising right up to his death in 1940. The book was finally published in a Moscow journal in 1966–67, but even then it was censored. Bulgakov's masterpiece fared better than his *Heart of a Dog,* which didn't see the light of day until 1987, more than 60 years after it was written.

Regimes change, and writers can fall into and out of favor. Alexander Solzhenitsyn lived long enough to fall in and out of official favor numerous times in the Soviet Union. When he was awarded the Nobel Prize in 1970, Solzhenitsyn wouldn't

Being deemed obscene is not the peril it once was. James Joyce was dogged by the squeamishness of others. In 1921, the husband of one of his typists found a section of a draft of *Ulysses* on the table, read it, tore it up, and burned it. In 1932, when *Ulysses* was banned in America for obscenity, Bennett Cerf moved to have the book legalized and had to insist on having it seized by the customs inspector in New York so it could be brought to trial. Barney Rosset, the publisher of Grove Press, won court battles over D. H. Lawrence's *Lady Chatterley's Lover*, William Burroughs's *Naked Lunch,* and some of the works of Henry Miller.

go to Sweden to collect the award in case he wasn't let back in the country. In the Nobel lecture given in the writer's absence, Solzhenitsyn talked about writers lost in the Gulag, the network of Soviet labor camps:

"Those who fell into that abyss already bearing a literary name are at least known, but how many were never recognized, never once mentioned in public? And virtually no one managed to return. A whole national literature remained there, cast into oblivion not only without a grave, but without even underclothes, naked, with a number tagged on to its toe. Russian literature did not cease for a moment, but from the outside it appeared a wasteland! Where a peaceful forest could have grown, there remained, after all the felling, two or three trees overlooked by chance."

When *Cancer Ward* was published in the United States, the Soviet Union declared Solzhenitsyn a "nonperson," and the first part of *The Gulag Archipelago* led to him being kicked out of the country. Mikhail Gorbachev rehabilitated Solzhenitsyn again, and in 1994 the writer returned to Russia.

This talk of censorship is not academic. A number of organizations: the American Library Association, the American Booksellers Association, and the American Booksellers Foundation for Free Expression, among others, sponsor "Banned Book Week," which celebrates freedom of expression and draws attention to the fact that books are challenged and banned today in the United States. Attempts have been made to take books like *To Kill a Mockingbird*, *The Adventures of Huckleberry Finn*, and *East of Eden* off library shelves. The five most-challenged books of 2002 were:

1. The Harry Potter series, by J. K. Rowling, for its focus on wizardry and magic.
2. The Alice series, by Phyllis Reynolds Naylor, for being sexually explicit, using offensive language, and being unsuited to age group.
3. *The Chocolate War,* by Robert Cormier, for using offensive language and being unsuited to age group.
4. *I Know Why the Caged Bird Sings,* by Maya Angelou, for sexual content, racism, offensive language, violence, and being unsuited to age group.
5. *Taming the Star Runner,* by S. E. Hinton, for offensive language.

Living Dangerously

In many parts of the world, a writer's life can be in danger because of something he or she has written. Free expression is guaranteed in few places.

In 1989 the British writer Salman Rushdie was sentenced to death by the Ayatollah Khomeini, the religious leader of Iran, because Rushdie's novel *The Satanic Verses* was allegedly blasphemous to Islam. The *fatwa* against Rushdie haunted him for years. Although the Iranian government disavowed the injunction to kill the writer, Rushdie continues to live a semisecret life.

The *fatwa* claimed other victims. People died in riots in India, the novel's Japanese translator was stabbed to death, and its Italian translator and Norwegian publisher were grievously wounded. And in countries from Tanzania to Thailand, the book was banned. Even at the end of the twentieth century, the power of the written word, even in fiction, was dramatically reaffirmed.

Since 1989 the advocacy group Human Rights Watch has made annual grants in the name of Lillian Hellman and Dashiell Hammett to persecuted writers around the world. Hellman's executors wanted to honor the playwright and her companion, who had been the subject of political interrogations themselves in the 1950s. In 2003 money was awarded to twenty-eight writers. Thirteen, from countries as various as Belarus, China, Eritrea, Liberia, Nepal, Ukraine, and Vietnam, asked not to be named for fear of reprisals.

The freedoms enjoyed by writers who can write freely without fear of reprisal are fragile and should be protected, nurtured, and celebrated.

CONCLUSION: THE WRITER

"History develops, art stands still. The novelist of the future will have to pass all the new facts through the old if variable mechanism of the creative mind."
—E. M. Forster

"My 39th birthday. A good year. I have begotten a fine daughter, published a successful book [*Put Out More Flags*], drunk 300 bottles of wine and smoked 300 or more Havana cigars."
—Evelyn Waugh

Perhaps the most prestigious forum afforded any writer is the lecture traditionally given during the ceremony in Stockholm that accompanies receipt of the Nobel Prize in literature. The speeches are a fascinating record of writers who usually will take that opportunity to talk broadly about the place of creativity in civilization.

"The ancient commission of the writer has not changed. He is charged with exposing our many grievous faults and failures, with dredging up to the light our dark and dangerous dreams for the purpose of improvement." —John Steinbeck (1962)

"Don't tell us what to believe, what to fear. Show us belief's wide skirt and the stitch that unravels fear's caul. You, old woman, blessed with blindness, can speak the language that tells us what only language can: how to see without pictures. Language alone protects us from the scariness of things with no names. Language alone is meditation." —Toni Morrison (1993)

"Writers should consider the condition of permanent controversiality to be invigorating, part of the risk involved in choosing the profession. It is a fact of life that writers have always and with due consideration and great pleasure spit in the soup of the high and mighty." —Günter Grass (1999)

"The writer cannot fill the role of the Creator so there is no need for him to inflate his ego by thinking that he is God." — Gao Xingjian (2000)

Writers in this echelon are international figures: ambassadors as well as artists whose prize often has a political dimension. There are other major writers of stature and extraordinary literary talent:

"A major writer combines these three—storyteller, teacher, enchanter—but it is the enchanter in him that predominates and makes him a major writer." —Vladimir Nabokov

"Every novel, like it or not, offers some answer to the question: What is human existence, and wherein does its poetry lie?" —Milan Kundera

"He is obviously the man who wrote his books—that is, he impresses you as an important enough personage for that."
—T. S. Eliot on James Joyce

The rare air that is breathed by the innovators and geniuses is too thin for most of us to flourish in. These writers are wonderful to read and discuss and follow but impossible to emulate. Reading a couple of pages of Nabokov or Joseph Conrad, for whom English was not even their first language, may make a beginning writer want to give up on the spot.

We should remember that there is no blueprint that describes a writer. Writers don't look alike, they don't act alike, and they certainly don't write like one another.

They can be Wallace Stevens, who worked for the Hartford Insurance Company for many years and wrote poetry he told few of his colleagues about. His first book was published when he was forty-four, the second when he was fifty-seven. They can be Margaret Edson, who won a Pulitzer Prize for her play *Wit* and went back to teaching kindergarten at a school in Atlanta. Or they can be any one of the writers featured in this book. Or they can be *you*, if you have it in you. It helps to decide what kind of writer you want to be. If you aspire to winning a Nobel Prize or writing a book that challenges the language, like *Ulysses*, you are setting yourself up for a tremendous challenge. Admire the great writers from afar and look toward the good writers—writers *you* think are good—and strive. Set a goal that's not so far in front of you that it is out of sight and work steadily toward it. You can set new goals again and again and successively challenge the writer that you are becoming.

"Your Writing Self is an evolving, creative force. If I could give you only one suggestion for nourishing a long and fulfilling writing life, it would be to respect this aspect of it." —Bonni Goldberg

"One must be stoic, one must develop a sense of humor. And, after all, there is the example of William Faulkner, who considered himself a failed poet; Henry James returning to prose fiction after the conspicuous failure of his play-writing career; Ring Lardner writing his impeccable American prose because he despaired of writing sentimental popular songs; Hans Christian Andersen perfecting his fairy tales since he was clearly a failure in other genres—poetry, play writing, life. One has only to glance at *Chamber Music* to see why James Joyce specialized in prose." —Joyce Carol Oates

"If I understood half of what I did or what I felt, I probably wouldn't waste my time writing. But I like the probing." —Terry McMillan

Remember also the rewards, both the tangible ones that come from creating a piece of work and the unseen benefits that accrue from the process.

"Writing is surely a delicious craft, and the writer is correctly envied by others, who must slave longer hours and see their labor vanish as they work, in the churning of human needs." —John Updike, *Odd Jobs*

"I wanted to write something to have something substantial to show for the end of the day's work. When you drive a bus all day there is nothing to show for it, apart from a little, very thin pay packet." —Magnus Mills

"Why does a man spend fifty years of his life in an occupation that is often painful? I once told a class I was teaching that writing is an intellectual contact sport, similar in some respects to football. The effort required can be exhausting, the goal unreached, and you are hurt on almost every play; but that doesn't deprive a man or a boy from getting peculiar pleasures from the game." —Irwin Shaw

Here's something you may well know already: you can't help yourself, there's no stopping you. What makes a writer, perhaps, is the obsession to write.

"Search for the reason that bids you write; find out whether it is spreading out its roots in the deepest places of your heart, acknowledge to yourself whether you would have to die if it were denied you to write. This above all—ask yourself in the stillest hour of the night: *must* I write? Delve into yourself for a deep answer. And if this should be affirmative, if you may meet this earnest question with a strong and simple '*I must*,' then build your life according to this necessity; your life even its most indifferent and slightest hour must be a sign of this urge and a testimony to it." —Rainer Maria Rilke, *Letters to a Young Poet*

"A writer is someone who cannot not write." —Sol Stein

"The difference between the writer and everyone else, however, is that instead of taking his retirement savings and traveling to the Far East with it or buying a Florida condo near a golf course, the writer hopes to spend it on time to write the books he has longed to write all his life." —Richard Curtis

"*Why* do we write? Here, too, I was lucky, for it never occurred to me that when it came to this question, one had a choice." —Imre Kertész, Nobel lecture (2002)

Bill Moyers: "Why do you write?"

Mark Doty: "Because I don't have a choice. Because it is the way I know what to think and feel."

"Asking whether you've got it, whether you should stick with writing or quit, is a little like asking if you should continue living. It's beside the point. No one can give you a reason to live if you don't have the will. For most writers, being unable to write is tantamount to suicide anyway." —Betsy Lerner

"With every sentence you write, you have learned something. It has done you good. It has stretched your understanding. I know that. Even if I knew for certain that I would never have anything published again, and would never make another cent from it, I would still keep on writing." —Brenda Ueland

The Last Word

"Find the time to write. Protect the time to write. Be inventive: get gorgons. Forget e-mail. Whatever it takes. Because you'll still need more time than there is, and also it's important to leave enough time to waste. That's one of the many reasons the stereotype of the writer with the bottle holds, though the creative wasting of time is not only more fun, but nobler. Don't let people persuade you to talk away your material, and don't let them persuade themselves that you are only another version of them. . . .

People who do not write will tell you that they haven't gotten around to it yet because they know they can. They just need to get the kids in school, hire a lawn service and spend weekends writing, re-cycle their notebooks into useable material, make a concerted effort to remember their dreams. It can be done tomorrow. Any time. They are just about to get to it—that thing that comes so naturally to all of us, that thing we've done all through school and with great élan in our love letters. The books they could write, their plots based on something that happened to them, that are more exciting than Le Carré's. Tomorrow. Tomorrow. I'll see you tomorrow.

They are not writing because they can. You are writing because you can't." —Ann Beattie

BIBLIOGRAPHY AND SOURCES

◎ ◎ ◎

Introduction

Baker: Baker, Nicholson. *U and I: A True Story*, New York: Random House, 1991.

Lamott: Lamott, Anne. *Bird by Bird: Some Instructions on Writing and Life*, New York: Pantheon Books, 1994.

Inspiration

Tolkien: Tolkien, J. R. R. *The Letters of J. R. R. Tolkien.* Selected and edited by Humphrey Carpenter. Boston: Houghton Mifflin, 1981.

Sontag: *Writers on Writing: Collected Essays from the New York Times.* New York: Times Books, 2001.

Gaines: *Conversations with Ernest Gaines.* Edited by John Lowe Jackson. Jackson: University Press of Mississippi, 1995.

Shields: *books.guardian.co.uk*

Achebe (American Academy): *amacad.org*

Achebe (Cary): Achebe, Chinua, *Home and Exile*, Oxford: OUP, 2000.

Stafford: Stafford, William. *Crossing Unmarked Snow: Further Views on the Writer's Vocation.* Ann Arbor: The University of Michigan Press, 1998.

Márquez: *themodernword.com*

Nin: *The Diary of Anaïs Nin. Volume V.* New York: Harcourt, Brace Jovanovich, 1974.

Simic: *cortlandreview.com*

Dunn: *english.lsu.edu*

Oates: *Writers on Writing, Op. cit.*

McDonnell: Jane Taylor McDonnell. *Living to Tell the Tale: A Guide to Writing Memoir.* New York: Penguin Books, 1998.

Murdock: Murdock, Maureen. *On Memoir and Memory.* New York: Seal Press, 2003.

Ashbery: *writenet.org*

Stanek: Stanek, Lou Willett. *Writing Your Life: Putting Your Past on Paper.* New York: Avon Books, 1996.

Sedaris: *ucsc.edu*

Welty: Welty, Eudora. *On Writing.* New York: Modern Library, 2002.

Lawrence: Lawrence, D. H., *Women in Love*, New York: Penguin Books, 1976.

Keller: *Poets and Writers*, March-April, 2002.

Stowe: Hendrick, Joan D. *Harriet Beecher Stowe: A Life.* New

York: Oxford University Press, 1994.

Rowling: *storiesfromtheweb.org*

Murakami: *salon.com*

Kaufman: *chasingthefrog.com*

Wolitzer: Wolitzer, Hilma. *The Company of Writers: Fiction Workshops and Thoughts on the Writing Life*. New York: Penguin Books, 2001.

Shelley: Shelley, Mary. *Frankenstein*. Norton Critical Edition. New York: W. W. Norton, 1996.

Curtis: Curtis, Richard. *Beyond the Bestseller: A Literary Agent Takes You Inside the Book Business*. New York: New American Library, 1989.

Spencer: Spencer, Stuart. *The Playwright's Guidebook*. London: Faber & Faber, 2002.

Roberts: *bookpage.com*

MacLeish: *Life*, July 14, 1961.

Trollope: Trollope, Anthony. *An Autobiography*. New York: Penguin Books, 1993.

Franzen: *newyorkmetro.com*

Rhodes: Rhodes, Jewell Parker. *Free Within Ourselves: Fiction Lessons for Black Authors*. New York: Main Street Books/Doubleday, 1999.

Reading and Writing

McCarthy: *New York Times*, April 19, 1992.

Bellow: Speech at the Nobel Prize Banquet, December 10, 1976.

Barthes: Barthes, Roland. *Image, Music, Text*. New York: Noonday Press, 1978.

Oates: Oates, Joyce Carol. *The Faith of a Writer*. New York: Ecco, 2003.

Sinclair: Sinclair, Upton. *The Autobiography of Upton Sinclair*. New York: Harcourt, Brace & World, 1962.

Carey: *books.guardian.co.uk*

Whitman: Whitman, Walt. *Leaves of Grass*. New York: Signet, 2000.

Stegner: Stegner, Wallace. *On Teaching and Writing Fiction*. New York: Penguin, 2002.

Mitchell: Mitchell, Joseph. *Up in the Old Hotel and Other Stories*. New York: Vintage Books, 1993.

García Márquez: García Márquez, Gabriel. *Living to Tell the Tale*. New York: Knopf, 2003.

Hornby: *barcelonareview.com*

Stevens: Stevens, Wallace. *Letters of Wallace Stevens*. Selected and edited by Holly Stevens. New York: Alfred A. Knopf, 1966.

Bradbury: Bradbury, Ray. *Zen in the Art of Writing*. Santa Barbara: Joshua Odell Editions, 1996.

Dove: *georgetown.edu*

McBain: *bookreporter.com*

Tremain: *book-club.co.nz*

Wilson: *Pittsburgh Post-Gazette*, March 28, 1999.

Higgins: Higgins, George V. *On Writing: Advice for Those Who Write to Publish (or Would Like To)*. New York: Henry Holt and Company, 1990.

Getting Started

Dufresne: Dufresne, John. *The Lie That Tells a Truth: A Guide to Writing Fiction*. New York: W. W. Norton & Co., 2003.

Roberts: *publishersweekly.com*

Clark: *powells.com*

Gordimer: *telegraph.co.uk*

Fleming: *sundayherald.com*

Griffin: *cnn.com*

Doctorow: quoted in E. L. Doctorow. *Ragtime*. New York: Modern Library, 1994.

Glass: *readinggroupguides.com*

Wesley: AP Wire, 12/31/2002.

Kingsolver: *kingsolver.com*

Welsh: *bombsite.com*

Pelecanos: *bookpage.com*

Audience

Allende: *womankindflp.org*

White: Strunk, William Jr., *The Elements of Style*. With revisions, an introduction and a chapter on writing by E. B. White. Fourth edition. Boston: Allyn and Bacon, 2000.

O'Neill: O'Neill, Eugene. *Selected Letters of Eugene O'Neill*. Edited by Travis Bogard and Jackson R. Bryer. New Haven: Yale University Press, 1988.

Hawthorne ("Some portions of the book …"): *uwm.edu*

—("It broke her heart…"): *newpaltz.edu*

Rabiner: Rabiner, Susan, and Alfred Fortunato. *Thinking Like Your Editor*. New York: W. W. Norton, 2002.

Melville: *melville.org*

Tolkien: Tolkien, *Op. cit.*

Lerner: Lerner, Betsy. *The Forest for the Trees: An Editor's Advice to Writers*. New York: Riverhead Books, 2000.

Johnson: Johnson, Alexandra. *Leaving a Trace: On Keeping a Journal*. New York: Little, Brown, 2001.

Spence: Spence, Linda. *Legacy: A Step-by-Step Guide to Writing Personal History*. Athens, OH: Swallow Press/Ohio University Press, 1997.

Rainer: Rainer, Tristine. *Your Life as a Story: Writing the New Autobiography*. New York: Putnam, 1997.

Stein: Stein, Sol. *How to Grow a Novel*. New York: St. Martin's Press, 1999.

Ford: *pbs.org*

Singer: Speech at the Nobel Prize Banquet, December 10, 1978.

Time and Space

Bowles: *The Writer's Chapbook*. Edited and with an introduction by George Plimpton. New York: Modern Library, 1999.

Lehane: *bookreporter.com*

Brande: Brande, Dorothea. *Becoming a Writer*. New York: Harcourt, Brace & Co., 1934.

Ackroyd: *books.guardian.co.uk*

Parker: *bookreporter.com*

Greene: Donaghy, Henry J., editor. *Conversations with Graham Greene*. Jackson: University Press of Mississippi, 1992.

Wharton: Lewis, R. W. B. *Edith Wharton: A Biography*. New York: Harper & Row, 1975.

Oates: Oates, *Op. cit.*

Paul: Paul, Noel C. "Shedding Writer's Block," *Christian Science Monitor*, November 21, 2001.

Thoreau: Thoreau, Henry David. *Walden and Civil Disobedience*. New York: Penguin Books, 1986.

Conroy: Paul, "Shedding Writer's Block," *Op. cit.*

Bradbury: *nationalbook.org*

Le Carré: *Entertainment Weekly*, Januaty 16, 2004.

Ellison: Ellison, Ralph. Introduction to the Thirtieth Anniversary Edition of *Invisible Man*. New York: Random House, 1982.

Valdes-Rodriguez: *publishersweekly.com*

Wilson: Wilson, Edmund. *Letters on Literature and Politics 1912-1972*. Edited by Elena Wilson. New York: Farrar, Straus & Giroux, 1977.

Franzen: *newyorkmetro.com*

London: Stone, Irving. *Jack London: Sailor on Horseback*. New York: New American Library, 1969.

Hardy, Thomas. *Far from the Madding Crowd*. Modern Library Edition. New York: Modern Library, 2001.

Foley: Foley, Mick. *Have a Nice Day!*, New York: HarperCollins, 1999.

Brontë: Gaskell, Elizabeth. *The Life of Charlotte Brontë*. New York: Penguin Books, 1998.

Caro: Sherman, Scott. "Caro's Way," *Columbia Journalism Review*, May-June 2002.

Form

Welty: *Conversations with Eudora Welty*. Edited by Peggy Whitman Prenshaw. Jackson: University of Mississippi Press, 1984.

Giles: *sfbg.com*

Heller: *theatlantic.com*

Poe: "The Philosophy of Composition," (1846). *eapoe.org*

Bellow: Bellow, Saul. Foreword to *Something to Remember Me By*. New York: Signet Books, 1991.

Mailer: Mailer, McElroy, Joseph. "Norman Mailer at Columbia." *Columbia* magazine, no. 6.

Porter: Porter, Katherine Anne. *Letters of Katherine Anne Porter*. Selected and edited by Isabel Bayley. New York: Atlantic Monthly Press, 1990.

Hills: Hills, Rust. *Writing in General and the Short Story in Particular*. Boston: Houghton Mifflin, 1977.

Miller: Miller, Henry. *Tropic of Cancer*. New York: Grove Press, 1989.

Pevear: Introduction to Tolstoy, Leo. *Anna Karenina*, translated by Richard Pevear and Larissa Volokhonsky, New York: Penguin Books, 2002.

Gornick: Gornick, Vivian. *The Situation and the Story: The Art of Personal Narrative*. New York: Farrar, Straus & Giroux, 2001.

Weldon: Weldon, Fay. *Auto da Fay: A Memoir*. New York: Grove Press, 2003.

Roy: *progressive.org*

Mailer: *Chicago Tribune*, 9/29/91.

Dillard: Dillard, Annie. *Living by Fiction*. New York: Harper & Row, 1982.

Parks: *ajc.com*

Labels and Categories

Rankin: *rampantscotland.com*

Asimov: Asimov, Isaac. *I, Asimov*. New York: Doubleday, 1994.

Shields: *guardian.co.uk*

Gaines: Jackson, *Op. cit.*

Gardner: Gardner, John. *The Art of Fiction*. New York: Alfred A. Knopf, 1984.

Woolf: Woolf, Virginia. *The Letters of Virginia Woolf: Volume I, 1882–1912*. Edited by Nigel Nicolson and Joanne Trautmann. New York: Harcourt Brace Jovanovich, 1975.

Glieck: *publishersweekly.com*

Tolkien: Tolkien, *Op. cit.*

Brooks: *scifi.com*

Asimov: Asimov, *Op. cit.*

Bear: Bear, Greg. *The Collected Stories of Greg Bear*. New York: Tor, 2002.

Turtledove: *chicon.org*

Straub: *locusmag.com*

Romance: *rwanational.org*

Grammar and Other Nuts and Bolts

Pinker: Pinker, Steven. *The Language Instinct*. New York: HarperPerennial, 2000.

Le Guin: Le Guin, Ursula K. *Steering the Craft: Exercises and Discussions on Story Writing for the Lone Navigator or the Mutinous Crew*. Portland, OR: The Eighth Mountain Press, 1988.

Vonnegut: Vonnegut, Kurt. *Bluebeard*. New York: Delacorte Press, 1987.

Parrish: Parrish, Thomas. *The Grouchy Grammarian*. New York: John Wiley & Sons, 2002.

Stevens: Stevens, *op. cit.*

Lawrence: *books.guardian.co.uk*

Faulkner: Blotner, Joseph and Noel Polk. Introduction to *William Faulker: Novels 1942–1954*. New York: Library of America, 1994.

Stein: Stein, Gertrude. *Lectures in America*. New York: Random House, 1935.

O'Conner: O'Conner, Patricia T., and Stuart Kellerman. *You Send Mail: Getting It Right When You Write Online*. New York: Harcourt, 2002.

Parris: Introduction to Fowler, H. W. and F. G. Fowler. *The King's English*. Oxford; U.K.: Oxford University Press, 2002.

Style

White: Strunk and White, *Op. cit.*

Strunk and White: *Op. cit.*

Mailer: *Pennsylvania Gazette*, May 1995.

Baker: Baker, Sheridan. *The Practical Stylist*. Seventh edition. New York: HarperCollins, 1990.

Ford: Allott, Miriam. *Novelists on the Novel*. New York: Columbia University Press, 1959. ·

Hemingway: Douglas, Ann. *Terrible Honesty: Mongrel Manhattan in the 1920s*. New York: Farrar, Straus & Giroux, 1995.

Higgins: Higgins, *Op. cit.*

Seidman: Seidman, Michael. *The Complete Guide to Editing Your Fiction*. Cincinnati: Writer's Digest Books, 2000.

Leonard: *elmoreleonard.com*

Sentences: Kane, Thomas S. *The Oxford Essential Guide to Writing*. New York: Berkeley, 2000.

O'Conner: O'Conner, Patricia T. *Woe Is I: The Grammarphobe's Guide to Better English in Plain English* (Expanded). New York: Riverhead Books, 2003.

See: See, Carolyn. *Making a Literary Life*. New York: Random House, 2001.

Bates: Bates, Jefferson D. *Writing with Precision*. Expanded edition. New York: Penguin Books, 2000.

Baker: Baker, *Op. cit.*

Moore: Moore, Marianne. *Predilections*. New York: The Viking Press, 1955.

Alexie: *english.uiuc.edu*

Trite Expressions: Skillin, Marjorie E., Robert M. Gay, et al. *Words into Type*. Upper Saddle River, NJ: Prentice Hall, 1974.

Twain: Letter to D. W. Bowser, March 1880.

Zinsser: Zinsser, William. *Writing to Learn*. New York: HarperResource, 1993.

Asimov: Asimov, *Op. cit.*

Naipaul: *Conversations with V. S. Naipaul*. Edited by Feroza Jussawalla. Jackson: University Press of Mississippi, 1997.

Welty: *Conversations*, *Op. cit.*

Burnett: Burnett, Hallie. *On Writing the Short Story*. New York: HarperPerennial, 1983.

Adams: Adams, Caroline Joy. *The Power to Write: A Writing Workshop in a Book*. York Beach, ME: Conari Press, 2003.

Gordon: Gordon, Karen Elizabeth. *The Transitive Vampire: A Handbook of Grammar for the Innocent, the Eager, and the Doomed*. New York: Times Book, 1984.

Leonard: *books.guardian.co.uk*

Plot and Character

Burroway: Burroway, Janet. *Writing Fiction: A Guide to Narrative Craft*. Sixth edition.

New York: Pearson Longman, 2002.

Atwood: *Mother Jones*, July-August 1997.

King: King, Stephen. *On Writing: A Memoir of the Craft*. New York: Scribner's, 2000.

Lamott: Lamott, *Op. cit.*

Block: Block, Lawrence. *Writing the Novel: From Plot to Print*. Cincinnati: Writer's Digest Books, 1985.

Bloom: Bloom, Harold. *The Western Canon*. New York: Riverhead Books, 1994.

King: King, *Op. cit.*

Le Carré: *bloc-online.com*

Tolkien: Tolkien, *Op. cit.*

Haddon: *powells.com*

Bowen: Bowen, Elizabeth. "Notes on Writing a Novel," *Collected Impressions*. New York: Alfred A. Knopf, 1950.

Giovanni: *writerswrite.com*

Mailer: Newsday, 9/21/75.

Banville: Boylan, Clare, editor. *The Agony and the Ego: The Art and Strategy of Fiction Writing Explored*. New York: Penguin, 1994.

Dibell: Dibell, Ansen. *Plot (Elements of Fiction Writing)*. Cincinnati: Writer's Digest Books, 1988.

Baker: *altx.com*

Connelly: Grafton, Sue, editor. *Writing Mysteries*. Cincinnati: Writer's Digest Books, 2002.

Wood: Wood, Monica. *Description (Elements of Fiction Writing)*. Cincinnati: Writer's Digest Books, 1999.

Conrad. Conrad, Barnaby. *Learning to Write Fiction from the Masters*. New York: Plume, 1996.

See: See, *Op. cit.*

Healy: Grafton, *Op. cit.*

Mortimer: *Paris Review,* 164, Winter 2003.

Adamson: Adamson, Lesley Grant. *Teach Yourself Writing Crime Fiction*. New York: McGraw-Hill/Contemporary Books, 2003.

Lukeman: Lukeman, Noah. *The Plot Thickens: Eight Ways to Bring Fiction to Life*. New York: St. Martin's Griffin, 2003.

Highsmith: Highsmith, Patricia. *Plotting and Writing Suspense Fiction*. New York: St. Martin's Press, 1990.

Telling the Story

Cather: Cather, Willa. *O Pioneers!* New York: Vintage Books, 1992.

Block: Block, *Op. cit.*

Brooks: Brooks, Terry. *Sometimes the Magic Works*. New York: Ballantine Books, 2003.

O'Connor: O'Connor, Flannery. *The Complete Stories*. Reissue edition. New York: Noonday Press, 1996.

Hillenbrand: *webdelsol.com*

Poe: Poe, *Op. cit.*

Gordimer: *telegraph.co.uk*

Szeman: Szeman, Sherri, "Who's Afraid of Point of View," in Leder, Meg, Jack Heffron, and the Editors of *Writer's Digest*.

The Complete Book of Novel Writing. Cincinnati: Writer's Digest Books, 2002.

Kesey: Kesey, Ken. *One Flew over the Cuckoo's Nest*. Edited By John Clark Pratt. New York: Viking Penguin, 1996.

Swift: Boylan, *Op. cit.*

Highsmith: Highsmith, *Op. cit.*

Le Guin: Le Guin, *Op. cit.*

Dufresne: Dufresne, *Op. cit.*

Poe: Poe, *Op. cit.*

Poe (*The Pit*): Poe, Edgar Allan: *The Complete Tales and Poems of Edgar Allan Poe*. New York: Vintage Books, 1987.

Happy families: Tolstoy, *Anna Karenina*, *Op. cit.*

Douglass: Douglass, Frederick. *Narrative of the Life of Frederick Douglass, An American Slave*. New York: Penguin Books, 1986.

Conrad: Conrad, Joseph. *Heart of Darkness*. New York: Penguin Books, 1995.

Dexter: Dexter, Pete. *Paris Trout*. New York: Random House, 1988.

Proust: Proust, Marcel. *In Search of Lost Time Volume One: Swann's Way*, translated by C. K. Scott Moncrieff and Terence Kilmartin, revised by D. J. Enright. New York: Modern Library, 1992.

Walker: Walker, Alice. *The Color Purple*. New York: Harcourt Brace Jovanovich, 1982.

Heller: Heller, Joseph. *Catch-22*. New York: Scribner's, 1996.

Pynchon: Pynchon, Thomas. *Gravity's Rainbow*. New York: The Viking Press, 1973.

Norris: Norris, Frank. *McTeague*. New York: Signet, 2003.

Ambler: Ambler, Eric. *A Coffin for Dimitrios*. New York: Vintage Books, 2001.

Schama: Schama, Simon. *Citizens: A Chronicle of the French Revolution*. New York: Alfred A. Knopf, 1989.

Mitchell: Mitchell, Joseph. *Joe Gould's Secret*. New York: Vintage Books, 1999.

Twain: *twainquotes.com*

Preston, Richard: *The Hot Zone*. New York: Random House, 1994.

Goldberg: Goldberg, Natalie. *Writing Down the Bones: Freeing the Writer Within*. Boston: Shambala Publications, 1986.

Stott: Stott, Bill. *Write to the Point and Feel Better About Your Writing*. New York: Columbia University Press, 1984.

Goldberg: Goldberg, Bonni. *Room to Write: Daily Invitations to a Writer's Life*. New York: Jeremy P. Tarcher/Putnam, 1996.

Lyon: Lyon, Elizabeth. *A Writer's Guide to Nonfiction*. New York: Perigee, 2003.

Ray and Remick: Ray, Robert J., and Jack Remick, *The Weekend Novelist Writes a Mystery*. New York: Dell, 1998.

Palahniuk: *publishersweekly.com*

Mamet: Mamet, David. *Three Uses of the Knife: On the Nature and Purpose of Drama.* New York: Columbia University Press, 1998.

Lamott: Lamott, *Op. cit.*

Stern: Stern, Jerome. *Making Shapely Fiction.* New York: W. W. Norton & Co., 2000.

Seidman: Seidman, *Op. cit.*

O'Hara ("Ninety Minutes Away") : O'Hara, John. *The Collected Short Stories of John O'Hara.* Edited and with an introduction by Frank MacShane, New York: Random House, 1984.

O'Hara: *Selected Letters of John O'Hara.* Edited by Matthew J. Bruccoli. New York: Random House, 1978.

Prose: *The Eleventh Draft: Craft and the Writing Life from the Iowa Writers' Workshop.* Edited by Frank Conroy. New York: HarperCollins, 1999.

Williams: Williams, Tennessee. In *Small Craft Warnings.* New York: New Directions, 1972.

Benedict: Benedict, Elizabeth. *The Joy of Writing Sex.* Revised edition. New York: Owl Books, 2002.

Kress: Kress, Nancy. *Beginnings, Middles, and Ends.* Cincinnati: Writer's Digest Books, 1993.

Koch: Koch, Stephen. *The Modern Library Writer's Workshop.* New York: The Modern Library, 2003.

Shields: *guardian.co.uk*

Keating: Keating, H. R. F. *Writing Crime Fiction.* New York: St. Martin's, 1996.

Heller: Heller, *Op. cit.*

Bernard: Bernard, André. *Now All We Need Is a Title: Famous Book Titles and How They Got That Way.* New York: W. W. Norton & Co., 1994.

O'Hara: *Selected Letters, Op cit.*

Gaines: Jackson, *Op. cit.*

Cisneros: *Poets and Writers,* September-October 2002.

O'Hara: Gooch, Brad. *City Poet: The Life and Times of Frank O'Hara.* New York: Alfred A. Knopf, 1993.

Rewriting

Bronte: Gaskell, *Op. cit.*

O'Hara: *Selected Letters, Op. cit.*

Poe: Poe, *The Philosophy of Composition*

Kennedy: *The Writer's Chapbook, Op. cit.*

Simic: *cortlandreview.com*

Schneider: Schneider, Pat. *Writing Alone and with Others.* New York: Oxford University Press, 2003.

Eliot: *Letters of T. S. Eliot. 1989–1922.* Edited by Valerie Eliot. New York: Harvest Books, 1990.

Hellman: Hellman, Lillian. *Three: An Unfinished Woman, Pentimento, Scoundrel Time.* Boston: Little, Brown, 1979.

McDermott: *albany.edu*

Heller: Sorkin, Adam J. *Conversations with Joseph Heller.* Jackson: The

University Press of Mississippi, 1998.

Irving: Irving, John. *The World According to Garp*. New York: Modern Library, 1998.

Huxley: Huxley, Aldous. *Brave New World*. New York: Perennial Library, 1969.

Fowles: Fowles, John. *The Magus*. Boston: Little, Brown, 1978 and New York: Modern Library, 1998.

Mamet: Mamet, *Op. cit.*

Productivity

Ford: Ford, Richard. *The Sportswriter*. Second edition. New York: Vintage, 1995.

Trollope: Trollope, *Op. cit.*

Tartt: *Poets and Writers*, November-December 2002.

Trollope: Trollope, *Op. cit.*

Twain: Twain, Mark. *The Autobiography of Mark Twain*. New York: Perennial, 2000.

Asimov: Asimov, *Op. cit.*

Harr: *Boston Phoenix*, August 18, 1995.

Pritchett: Pritchett, V. S. *A Cab at the Door and Midnight Oil*. New York: Modern Library, 1994.

Hemingway: Meyers, Jeffrey. *Hemingway: A Biography*. New York: Harper & Row, 1985.

Michener: *Reader's Digest*, 1962.

Yeats: *The Collected Letters of W. B. Yeats. Volume III*. Edited by John Kelly and

Ronald Schuchard. New York: Oxford University Press, 1994.

Vidal: Vidal, Gore. *Washington, D.C.* New York: Modern Library, 1999.

Lee: Newquist, Roy, editor. *Counterpoint*. Chicago: Rand McNally, 1964.

Degree of Difficulty

Angell: Strunk and White, *Op. cit.*

Lebowitz: *Playboy*, July 1984.

Le Carré: *bloc-online.com*

Wister: *Owen Wister Out West: His Journals and Letters*. Edited by Fanny Kemble Wister. Chicago: University of Chicago Press, 1958.

McMillan: *seeingblack.com*

Lee: *princeton.edu*

Porter: Porter, *Op. cit.*

Wolff: *alumni.utah.edu*

Stewart: Stewart, James B. *Follow the Story: How to Write Successful Nonfiction*. New York: Touchstone, 1998.

Yeats: Yeats, *Op. cit.*

Melville: *melville.org*

Goldberg: Goldberg, Natalie. *Thunder and Lightning: Cracking Open the Writer's Craft*. New York: Bantam Books, 2001.

Berg: Berg, Elizabeth. *Escaping into the Open: The Art of Writing True*. New York: HarperCollins, 1999.

Price: *Conversations with Reynolds Price*. Edited by Jefferson Humphries. Jackson: University Press of Mississippi, 1991.

Cornwell: *ivillage.co.uk*

Doyle: *sherlockholmesonline.org*

Austen: Austen, Jane. *Jane Austen's Letters to Her Sister Cassandra and Others*, collected and edited by R.W. Chapman, 2nd ed., Oxford: OUP, 1952.

Journalism

Talese: Talese, Gay. *The Kingdom and the Power*. New York: New American Library, 1969.

Woolf: Woolf, *Op. cit.*

Wilde: *New Dictionary of Quotations*.

Neal and Brown: Neal, James M., and Suzanne S. Brown. *Newswriting and Reporting*. Ames: The Iowa State University Press, 1976.

Hamill: Hamill, Pete. *News Is a Verb: Journalism at the End of the Twentieth Century*. New York: Ballantine, 1998.

Dreiser: Dreiser, Theodore. *Newspaper Days*. Edited by T. D. Nostwich. Philadelphia: University of Pennsylvania Press, 1991.

Dickens: Forster, John. *The Life of Charles Dickens*. London: Chapman and Hall, 1872.

Neal and Brown: Neal and Brown, *Op. cit.*

Dreiser: Dreiser, *Op. cit.*

Poston: Hanke, Kathleen A., editor. *Ted Poston: A First Draft of History*. Athens: The University of Georgia Press, 2002.

Dreiser: Dreiser, *Op. cit.*

Germond: Germond, Jack W. *Fat Man in a Middle Seat: Forty Years of Covering Politics*. New York: Random House, 1999.

Ford: Ford, Richard. *The Sportswriter, Op. cit.*

Wilson: Wilson, *Op. cit.*

Bombeck: Braden, Maria. *She Said What? Interviews with Women Newspaper Columnists*. Lexington: The University Press of Kentucky, 1993.

Reston: Stacks, John F. *Scotty: James B. Reston and the Rise and Fall of American Journalism*. New York: Little, Brown, 2003.

Talese: Talese, *Op. cit.*

CPJ figures: *CPJ.org*

Pyle: Andrews, Allan R. *American Reporter*, April 15, 1999.

Pyle (Waskow): Pyle, Ernie. "The Death of Captain Waskow," January 10, 1944.

Pyle obituary: *New York Times*, April 19, 1945.

Poetry

Garrison: Moyers, Bill. *Fooling with Words: A Celebration of Poets and Their Craft*. New York: William Morrow, 1999.

Graham: *pbs.org*

Oliver: Oliver, Mary. *A Poetry Handbook*. New York: Harvest, 1994.

Pinsky: Moyers, *Op. cit.*

Piercy: *Writers on Writing, Op. cit.*

Williams: *Slamnation.com*

Wooldridge: Wooldridge, Susan. *poemcrazy: Freeing Your Life with Words*. New York: Clarkson Potter, 1996.

Collins: *Terraincognita.com*

Packard: Packard, William. *The Art of Poetry Writing*. New York: St. Martin's Press, 1992.

Stevens: Stevens, *Op. cit.*

Plumly: *theatlantic.com*

Bugeja: Bugeja, Michael J. *The Art and Craft of Poetry*. Cincinnati: Writer's Digest Books, 1994.

Rukeyser: Rukeyser, Muriel. *The Life of Poetry*. New York: Current Books, 1949.

Hillyer: Hillyer, Robert. *In Pursuit of Poetry*. New York: McGraw-Hill, 1960.

Rich: *progressive.org*

Boland: *caffeinedestiny.com*

Oliver: Oliver, *Op. cit.*

Frost: Frost, Robert. *Interviews with Robert Frost*, edited by Edward Connery Latham. New York: Holt, Rinehart & Winston, 1966.

Oliver: Oliver, *Op. cit.*

Playwriting

Murdoch: *The Writer's Chapbook*. Edited and with an introduction by George Plimpton. New York: Modern Library, 1999.

Parks: *telegraph.co.uk*

Updike: Updike, John. *Odd Jobs: Essays and Criticism*, New York: Alfred A. Knopf, 1991.

Bloom: Bloom, Harold. *The Western Canon*. New York: Riverhead Books, 1994.

Egri: Egri, Lajos. *The Art of Dramatic Writing*. New York: Kensington, 1985.

McLaughlin: McLaughlin, Buzz. *The Playwright's Process: Learning the Craft from Today's Leading Dramatists*. New York: Back Stage Books, 1977.

Hull: Hull, Raymond. *How to Write a Play*. Cincinnati: Writer's Digest Books, 1983.

Esslin: Esslin, Martin. *An Anatomy of Drama*. New York: Hill and Wang, 1977.

Hellman: Hellman, *Op. cit.*

Wilder: *Playwrights on Playwriting*. Edited by Tony Cole. New York: Hill and Wang, 1961.

Pike and Dunn: Pike, Frank, and Thomas G. Dunn. *The Playwright's Handbook*. Revised and updated edition. New York: Plume, 1996.

Priestley: Priestley, J. B. *The Art of the Dramatist*. London: Heinemann, 1957.

Osborne: *Playwrights on Playwriting, Op cit.*

Grebanier: Grebanier, Bernard. *Playwriting: How to Write for the Theater*. New York: Thomas Y. Crowell Company, 1961.

Wasserstein: *ntcp.org*

Williams: Miller, J. William. *Modern Playwrights at Work*. New York: Samuel French, Inc., 1968.

O'Neill: O'Neill, *Op. cit.*

Screenwriting

Goldman: Goldman, William. *Which Lie Did I Tell?* New York: Pantheon, 2001.

Russo: *usatoday.com*

Foote. Foote, Horton. *To Kill a Mockingbird, Tender Mercies, and The Trip to Bountiful. Three Screenplays.* New York: The Grove Press, 1989.

Faulkner, William. *Selected Letters of William Faulkner,* edited by Joseph Blotner. New York: Random House, 1977.

Gilles: Gilles, D. B. *The Screenwriter Within: How to Turn the Movie in Your Head into a Salable Screenplay.* New York: Three Rivers Press, 2000.

O'Hara: *Selected Letters, Op. cit.*

Field: Field, Syd. *Screenplay: The Foundation of Screenwriting.* New York: DTP, 1984.

DiMaggio: DiMaggio, Madeline. *How to Write for Television.* New York: Fireside, 1993.

Howard and Mabley: Howard, David and Edward Mabley. *The Tools of Screenwriting.* New York: St. Martin's Press, 1995.

Field: *Op. cit.*

McKee: Parker, Ian. "The Real McKee," *New Yorker,* October 20, 2003.

Flinn: Flinn, Denny Martin. *How Not to Write a Screenplay.* Los Angeles: Lone Eagle Publishing, 1999.

Dancyger and Rush: Dancyger, Ken, and Jeff Rush. *Alternative Scriptwriting: Successfully Breaking the Rules.* Third Edition. Burlington, MA: Focal Press, 2001.

Tarantino: *Quentin Tarantino: Interviews.* Edited by Gerald Peary. Jackson: The University Press of Mississippi, 1998.

Mamet: *mindspring.com*

Adams: Adams, Max. *The Screenwriter's Survival Guide.* New York: Warner Books, 2001.

Crowe: *theonion.com*

Chabon: *Salon.com*

Writing Courses

Wolff: *alumni.utah.edu. continuum*

King: King, *Op. cit.*

McCarthy: *New York Times,* April 19, 1992.

Iowa: Writers' Workshop, University of Iowa, "Brochure."

Kerouac: *The Portable Jack Kerouac.* Edited by Ann Charters. New York: The Viking Press, 1995.

Graham: *poets.org*

Canin: *stanfordalumni.org*

O'Connor: *The Complete Stories, Op. cit.*

West: West, Paul. *Master Class: Scenes from a Fiction Workshop.* New York: Harcourt, 2001.

Gardner: Gardner, John. *On Becoming a Novelist.* New York: W. W. Norton & Co., 1999.

Stegner: Stegner, *Op. cit.*

Gardner: Gardner, *Op. cit.*
McCarthy: *New York Times Book Review*, April 19, 1992.
Frost: Frost, *Op. cit.*
Phillips: *jayneannephillips.com*

Publishers and Publication

Steinbeck: *Newsweek*, December 24, 1962.
Austen: Austen, *Op. cit.*
Von Mehren: *Editors on Editing: What Writers Need to Know About What Editors Do.* Selected, edited, and with Commentary and Preface by Gerald Cross. New York: Grove Press, 1993.
Meredith: Meredith, Scott. *Writing to Sell.* Fourth Edition. Cincinnati: Writer's Digest Books, 1995.
Simon: Simon, Rachel. *The Writer's Survival Guide.* Cincinnati: Writer's Digest Books, 1997.
Lahiri: *pifmagazine.com*
Bogen: Bogen, Nancy. *How to Write Poetry.* Third edition. New York: Macmillan, 1991.
Leland: Leland, Christopher, T. *The Art of Compelling Fiction.* Cincinnati: Writer's Digest Books, 1998.
Ashmead: *publishersweekly.com*
Smith: Smith, Datus C., Jr. *A Guide to Book Publishing.* Revised edition. Seattle: University of Washington Press, 1989.
Cerf: Cerf, Bennett. *At Random: The Reminiscences of Bennett Cerf.* New York: Random House, 1977.

Porter: Porter, *Op. cit.*
Howard: *Editors on Editing. Op. cit.*
Perkins: Berg, A. Scott. *Max Perkins: Editor of Genius.* New York: Dutton, 1978.
Epstein: Epstein, Jason. *Book Business: Publishing Past, Present, and Future.* New York: W. W. Norton & Co., 2001.
West: West, *Op. cit.*
Updike: Updike, *Op. cit.*
Sorrentino: *publishersweekly.com*
Frame: Frame, Janet. *An Autobiography.* New York: George Brazillier, 1991.
Ross: Howry, Michelle, editor. *Agents, Editors, and You: The Insider's Guide to Getting Your Book Published.* Cincinnati: Writer's Digest Books, 2002.

Agents

Porter: Porter, *Op. cit.*
O'Hara: *Letters, Op. cit.*
O'Neill: O'Neill, *Op. cit.*
McDermott: *The Book That Changed My Life: Interviews With National Book Award Winners and Finalists.* Edited by Neil Baldwin. New York: Modern Library, 2002.
Hillenbrand: *webdelsol.com*

Getting Paid

Johnson: *A New Dictionary of Quotations.* Selected and edited by H. L. Mencken. New York: Alfred A. Knopf, 1982.

Austen: Austen, *Op. cit.*
King: King, *Op. cit.*
Faulkner: *Letters*, *Op. cit.*
O'Hara: *Letters*, *Op. cit.*
Stevens: Stevens, *Op. cit.*
Llosa: Llosa, Mario Vargas. *Letters to a Young Novelist.* New York: Picador, 2003.
Stevens: Stevens, *Op. cit.*
Mill, John Stuart. *Autobiography.* New York: Penguin Books, 1990.

Occupational Hazards

Dardis: Dardis, Tom. *The Thirsty Muse: Alcohol and the American Writer.* New York: Ticknor & Fields, 1989.
Lamott: Lamott, *Op. cit.*
Wolfe: Kesey, *Op. cit.*
Lerner: Lerner, *Op. cit.*
Martin: Martin, Steve. *Writing is Easy.* New York: Hyperion Books, 1998.
Frank: Frank, Stephen. *The Pen Commandments: A Guide for the Beginning Writer.* New York: Pantheon Books, 2003.
Shaughnessy: Shaughnessy, Susan. *Walking on Alligators: A Book of Meditations for Writers.* San Francisco: HarperSanFrancisco, 1993.
Morrison: *Conversations with Toni Morrison.* Edited by Danielle Taylor-Guthrie. Jackson: University Press of Mississippi, 1994.
Hemingway: Meyers, Jeffrey. *Hemingway: A Biography.* New York: Harper & Row, 1985.

Chabon: Chabon, Michael. *Wonder Boys.* New York: Picador Books, 1996.
Plotz: *slate.com*
Mallon: Mallon, Thomas. *Stolen Words.* New York: Harvest, 2001.
Drew University: *depts.drew.edu*
Conroy: *bookpage.com*
Mailer: *Michigan Quarterly Review*, Summer 1985.
Mahoney: *publishersweekly.com*
Asimov: Asimov, *Op. cit.*
Fischer: *telegraph.co.uk*
Camus: *Boston Globe*, October 30, 1995.
Solzhenitsyn: Nobel Prize Lecture, 1970.
Challenged books: *ala.org*

Conclusion: The Writer

Forster: Forster, E. M. *Aspects of the Novel.* New York: Harcourt, 1927.
Waugh: *The Diaries of Evelyn Waugh.* Edited by Michael Davie. Boston: Little, Brown, 1976.
Steinbeck: Speech at the Nobel Prize Banquet, December 10, 1962.
Morrison: Nobel Lecture, December 7, 1993.
Grass: Nobel Lecture, December 7, 1999.
Gao Xingjian: Nobel Lecture, December 7, 2000.
Nabokov: Nabokov, Vladimir. *Lectures on Literature.* Edited by Fredson Bowers. New York: Harcourt Brace Jovanovich, 1980.

Kundera: Kundera, Milan. *The Art of the Novel*. New York: Grove Press, 1988.

Eliot: Eliot, *Op. cit.*

Goldberg: Goldberg, *Op. cit.*

Oates: Oates, *Op. cit.*

McMillan: *writingforum.com*

Updike: Updike, *Op. cit.*

Mills: *bbc.co.uk*

Shaw: Shaw, Irwin. *Short Stories: Five Decades*. New York: Dell, 1983.

Rilke: Rilke, Rainer Maria, *Letters to a Young Poet*, translated by M. D. Herter Norton, revised edition. New York, W. W. Norton & Co., 1993.

Stein: Stein, *Op. cit.*

Curtis: Curtis, *Op. cit.*

Kertész: Nobel Lecture, December 7, 2002.

Doty: Moyers, *Op. cit.*

Lerner, Lerner, *Op. cit.*

Ueland: Ueland, Brenda. *If You Want to Write*. St. Paul: Graywolf Press, 1987.

Beattie: *Letters to a Fiction Writer*. Edited by Frederick Busch. New York: W. W. Norton & Co., 1999.

ACKNOWLEDGMENTS

◎ ◎ ◎

Every book is a collaborative venture. The idea for The Writer's Mentor *came from Jena Pincott at Random House, and her editorial expertise throughout the process has been invaluable. I am very grateful to Sheryl Stebbins for thinking of me for the project. Thanks also to my friends Ruth Fecych and Bud Kliment for their help.*

I would also like to acknowledge the contributions of Laura Magzis, the copyeditor; Tina Malaney for the interior design; Nora Rosansky for the cover; Beth Levy, the managing editor; and Jeanne Kramer, publisher of Random House Reference. Thank you to all.

Kara Welsh is my mentor, and this is for her, and for Lindsay, and for Sam.

ASK A MENTOR

◎ ◎ ◎

In the spirit of the Writer's *Mentor*, Ian Jackman will answer your questions (or point you in the right direction for answers) about writing for publication.

Visit www.ianjackman.com

The web site also includes information on other books in the *Mentor* series. From *The Artist's Mentor*:

> "Why make art? Because I think there's a child's voice in every artist saying: 'I am here. I am somebody. I made this. Won't you look?'" —Chuck Close

Ian Jackman is a writer, ghostwriter, editor, and former managing director of the Modern Library.

INDEX

◎ ◎ ◎